CHASING
woodstock

FINDING THE COST OF FREEDOM
by RON EVANS

3 days of peace & music

EUPRAX BOOKS

Published by: EupraxBooks

An imprint of EupraxMedia
N. Clarendon, Vt 05759

ISBN# 978-0-9914166-0-8

E-mail: woodstockprogramproject@yahoo.com

Library of Congress
Control Number #2014933773

Graphic Design & photography by; Linda K Evans, except where noted.

Printed in the U.S.A.

In memory of Sidney Eckstein Evans and Janet White Evans

With admiration and love for Professor Milton White

For my lifelong adventure with the actinic, erudite design artist Linda Kiracofe Evans who can hide a greyhound in almost anything she creates.

TABLE OF CONTENTS

Prologue i

Foreword iii

Chapter 1: Angel Eyes 1

Chapter 2: Paul Newman & Phinius T. Barnum 7

Chapter 3: Kent State & "Mother" Miami 13

Chapter 4: "Pride in our Past" 23

Chapter 5: The Real Doral Country Club 27

Chapter 6: Discovering "New Connecticut" 35

Chapter 7: From Family Farm to Water Feature 45

Chapter 8: Reaching for the Stars 53

    Ben, Jerry, Arlo, & The Band 55

    Johnny Winter 60

    Joan Baez: Part One 62

    The Tee 67

    Richie Havens 69

    Crosby Stills & Nash 73

    Yasgur's Farm 1994 77

    Grateful Dead 86

    Leavin' the Light On 90

    David Clayton Thomas: Blood Sweat, & Tears 93

    David Crosby 96

    Leslie West: Mountain 99

    Ravi & Annoushka Shankar 101

    Joan Baez: Part Two 105

    Melancholy Memoirs of the Dead 106

    Paving Paradise: Putting up a Parking Lot 109

    John Sebastian: A Lovin' Spoonful 112

    John Fogerty & Family 114

Jocko & Donny: Sha-Na-Na 117

Elliott Landy: Landyvision 118

Trump gets "Fired" 122

Ten Years After 127

Grace Slick: Jefferson Airplane 129

Iron Butterfly 133

The Who 137

The Longest Winter 142

See Me, Feel Me 147

Everyday People 151

Country Joe 154

Joe Cocker: Part One 157

Joe Cocker: Part Two 159

Joe Cocker: Part Three 169

Heroes of Woodstock: 40th Anniversary Tour 173

Gilles Malkine: Tim Hardin Band 181

Alan Cooper: Sha-Na-Na 184

Michael Lang: Woodstock Producer 188

Denny Greene: Sha-Na-Na 190

Joshua White: The Joshua White Show 194

The Safka Soliloquy 200

Just Pen Pals 204

Eva's Secret 208

Swinging out with Mark Kapner 213

Chapter 9: Finding the Cost of Freedom or the Answer 217

Chapter 10: Arm up with Love, and come from the Shadows — Joan Baez . . 229

Chapter 11: Four Dead in Ohio — May 4th, 1970 233

Chapter 12: E=MC² 239

prologue

The celebration at "The Garden" was the confluence of many ideals that reached an apex for my generation at Yasgur's farm during the summer of 1969. The burning desire for racial and sexual equality, the secularization of social and ethical free thought and expression, along with the realization that people from all realms of the human condition could come together, share peace, love and music, celebrate the death of hatred, bigotry and senseless war, social injustice and ecologically disastrous materialism, and in doing so, find a voice that could lead to a new and more open social experiment for America. Well, we got the new social experiment alright. The corporatization and homogenization of Main Street, the opening of the Wall Street and Industrial/Military financial floodgates and the prosthelization of a fear-driven theosophy would instead thrust our nation back into the dark ages and to the precipice of bankruptcy. Peace, love and music would have to wait ... but, for how long?

Ron

I've been a visual artist all my life ... I equate Rock & Roll with periods in art history.

Folk music = social commentary.

Motown = civil rights

Woodstock = a cathartic demonstration; an act of rebellion.

I think it's been Ron's chase but I see it as an act of social art. How have the artists changed since that historic weekend? What is their retrospective and why do so many seem to make excuses for what they did and who they were? The Original Woodstock Program Project, which this book chronicles, has provided Ron and me with an exclusive and rare opportunity to share this historic concert program with the artists who defined our generation and to see how, along the way, they have used their fame or obscurity to help others find their voice. The result may surprise you.

Linda K Evans

Foreword

Foreword: by Ron Evans and Yvonne Daley.

I didn't go to Woodstock. Word of the big party had made its way to my home in Connecticut, where I, like so many of my generation, was being kept alive by music, the harbinger of adventure, the connective thread that linked me to like-minded kids coast to coast As the weekend ensued and news of the goings-on at Max Yasgur's farm filtered through my requisite obligations – the party on the jammed highway; stories of wild naked dancing; drugs, of course, psychedelics; and the music – I wished some more, then put my wishes away. I'd told my parents I would stay home and work so I stayed home and worked. The weekend rolled away. North of Woodstock, New York, my parents were making their way back from Canada, when they stopped to gas up in Lake George ... they'd been seeing the painted vans, the painted children in tie-dye and flowers, making their own way home, traveling the road. There at the gas station was another gaggle of long-haired, blissed-out kids. They were out of gas and out of money. My parents, true to their nature, gave them $5.00 – enough to fill their tank (remember when gas cost 35 cents a gallon?) and told them about their son back home who had wanted to go to Woodstock but elected to stay home and work.. Just as they were pulling out of the station, *one of the kids, a girl with whom my mother had made fast friends, jumped into the back of the van, grabbed something, then ran after my folks. "Here, give this to your son," she said. What she held was a treasure, although she didn't know that. It was the official Woodstock program, a gem of art, photography and graphics that highlighted all of the planned performers. Few people attending the concert ever saw it. The delivery truck bearing boxes of these programs was among the thousands of vehicles that got stuck in the monumental traffic jam along the Interstate, a jam caused by the sea of kids who didn't stay home but took the road toward ecstasy or misery, depending on their version of that memorable weekend. The programs finally arrived late Sunday evening, near the end of the concert. With few exceptions, the boxes got dumped in the biblical mud that Woodstock attendees still talk about, mud that ruined most of the volumes. Thus began my quest. I've been chasing that legendary event for 45 years, chasing the dream of a shared planet, a less materialistic lifestyle, the love message – all that and more, armed with the official Woodstock program my parents gave me upon their return. I may have missed Woodstock but in the intervening years, I have met and shared stories with most of the artists who were there. With my treasured program as my passport, I have journeyed from concert to private home to radio station and beyond, accompanied by my official photographer and beautiful wife, Linda, showing the program to the artists who are presented so vividly on its pages – most of whom did not know it existed – gathering their stories and autographs. Come with me, my fellow adventurer, as I tell you of my travels back to what I missed and my journey forward, a journey of innocence lost and of renewed hope.*

chapter one
ANGEL EYES

For too few years, back in the 90s, August was the month that Linda and I got to play aunt and uncle to my younger brother's kid, Catherine (Cat).. The week or so in Vermont, away from her Connecticut home, seemed our only real, one on one, bonding opportunity. In 1995, "Cat's" visit coincided with our second and probably last chance to catch up with the famed Woodstock guitarist, Carlos Santana. Arrangements for the August tour stop at the Saratoga Performing Arts Center had already been made through management, complete with complimentary passes awaiting us at SPAC's Will Call window. I don't think our nine-year-old niece had ever been to an ear-popping rock concert before. Would she even know or care who Carlos Santana was anyway? I figured her answer would be the usual, "Whatever!" She had no good reason to trust us this time around. We'd pulled so many Halloween style tricks and stunts on her as a child, that we had little hope she'd consent. But consent she did. It was time to pack the earplugs.

Jeff Beck, the former member of the Yardbirds, whom Rolling Stone magazine ranks as the fifth greatest guitarist of all times, was opening for Santana. Both were on our list of artists who had been scheduled to appear at Yasgur's Farm on August 15, 16 and 17, 1969 at an event that would come to be known as Woodstock. The Aquarian Exposition, that pivotal event that marked that apex of the counter-culture peace movement for a baby boom generation, was, after all, the force that brought us all together on this day, 26 years later. As guests of Santana, I sensed there was a slim chance that circumstances would allow us to catch up with both artists. After a half dozen years doing what we'd dubbed The Original Woodstock Program Project, we had learned that once you cross that security line between ticket holder and credentialed pass holder or tour guest, you became part of a different dynamic, a different energy, a different set of rules and you'd better be tenacious enough to handle the twists and turns.

On this night, it seemed that all of the administration and security at SPAC, where so many of our previous meet-ups had occurred, were aware that we would be crossing that line. Instead of arriving mid afternoon, during sound check, which was our M.O., we entered the secure zone, stage left, an hour or so before the show. I checked in, as I had dozens of times before, with Charlie, or Bill Darcey, or whoever was new to the backstage security post. In the early days of the project, my friends at SPAC would do what they could to introduce us to either the artists themselves or more often to the road manager who would become the key player in deciding our fate. All those dynamics were moot; my pass was secured firmly to my official Woodstock Program T-shirt.

It was precisely that tee that brought us back to this very spot almost two years to the date after a snafu that might have made the national news ended in my sitting in Carlos Santana's dressing room eating fresh fruit and shoot'n the shit with his brother Jorge. I flashed back to that moment, the fright that had me stomping around, threatening to call the state police to report a theft at the concert, by none other than the star of the show, Carlos Santana. My patience had worn thin waiting for a band member who had guaranteed me he would take my prized Woodstock program to Carlos personally, get it signed and bring it right back. After 20 minutes and no sign of either the band member or my prized, one-of-a-kind artifact, my frustration became fear, my fear grew contagious and loud. Either I or someone else was going to get arrested that night if someone didn't tell me what was going on or better yet hand back the program I had never let out of my sight, till then. A zero tolerance security guard held me back as I anxiously paced back and forth down the busy, after show, backstage hallway intersection just shouting distance from the band's dressing rooms. Eventually another band member heard my threat and asked me what had happened. "Come with me," he said, music to my ears as we strode past the security guard and maybe fifty feet down the hall to Carlos' dressing room and there was brother Jorge, feet up on the coffee table, eating fruit and paging through my prized possession. The catharsis was immeasurable; I blurted out my relief, "Holy shit, you scared the crap out of me, Man, am I glad you have it." I remember Jorge's answer: "Sorry, man. Hey, this thing is amazing!"

I left the program in Jorges' possession as we discussed the details of the project, ate some fruit and the time flew by. I asked him if he or Carlos had ever seen a copy of this rare and historic document before. He gave me the answer I was hoping for. They had not. Carlos was unable to join us, he explained, as he was involved in business negotiations. However, true to his word, the band member whom I engaged to acquire the prized signature was in fact successful, having added most of the band members' signatures as well. Jorge was warm, personal and engaging. We left the dressing room at close to midnight, feeling so privileged to have been there and yet, after all these years, disappointed that, having been so close, we still hadn't met the legend himself.

Jeff Beck had finished his intro. I left Linda and Cat at the seats Carlos had given us this second time around and decided to see if I could make my way up to the first few rows reserved for band members and guests. At past events, this and backstage access was vehemently denied until after the show. No such interference occurred this time around. I sat in the front row and watched the start of the Santana set and when it came time to move backstage, security stepped aside. Walking right past Beck, I made my way back to the "scene of the crime" intersection, pulled up a plastic milk crate, and joined three others who were just shoot'n the breeze. The stage door was ten feet away. The percussion and bass shook the concrete walls and floor, the floor shook the crate, the crate shook my whole body. One of my new-found backstage associates turned out to be Carlos' road manager, another the keyboardist's girlfriend. I tried to contribute to the banter but spent most of my time observing drinks being shuffled back and forth to the stage. Suddenly, the band began playing a song that was a favorite of the girl to my right and she announced she was going out on stage to dance. Half of our little milk carton group jumped up and headed for the door. Mustering all my nerve, I turned to the tour manager and asked if he thought it would be okay if I joined them. He looked at my credentials, looked me straight in the eye and announced, "Dude, you can go anywhere you want, you have ALL ACCESS!"

I hit the stage, trying not to look completely out of place. I was stage right, directly behind the keyboard player and his dancing hottie. My sensory receptors were on overload as I scanned about the thunderous scene. A three-story light show was to my left, a screaming crowd of 15,000 fans on my right and Mr. Carlos Santana was performing center stage, about 15 to 20 feet away. I jumped in for the dance; no time to be shy. Even after losing my dance partners, the urge to soak it all in kept me riveted to my position as Santana offered up yet another classic guitar riff and I had to pinch myself just to make sure it was all really happening.

As the concert was winding down, I worked my way back to the audience. "Would you like to meet Carlos," I asked Catherine. She and Linda were seated about 20 rows from stage. Sure, she would but more important she gushed, "Uncle Ron, were you just on stage dancing? It looked like you up there!"

"Come with me right now," I said as we skirted the crowd and headed for the parking lot where the tour buses and tractor trailers provided cover and a shortcut backstage. Charlie was on security and was already tuned into what was happening. It was back to "Hollywood & Vine" the famous hallway intersection where you never knew who you would literally bump into.

Our moment had finally come. I was standing face to face with the icon. He received us as if he were expecting us for a late night dinner. I introduced my wife and niece. The funny thing was that it seemed so comfortable. Carlos was a gentleman in his environment. He extended his hand to each of us and when Cat drew close, he looked at her exuberant expression and said, " Catherine, you have angel eyes." We each posed for pictures and I gave Carlos the official Woodstock Program Project T-shirt that I had promised. He was visibly intrigued with the black and white motif depicting the Woodstock dove and guitar and list of all the artists, among them The Santana Blues Band.

The moment that had taken years to create was in an instant past. I had been the ALL ACCESS guest of the one and only Carlos Santana. There was only thing standing in the way of making this the perfect Woodstock program experience. Two hours earlier, I had walked right past Jeff Beck backstage but my prized document was in safekeeping with Cat and Linda, out in the audience, and therefore I could not get his signature. Chasing Woodstock was becoming as much about missed opportunities as about sharing and discovery. It was approaching midnight as we exited the SPAC parking lot and we all realized it had been a lifetime since our last food. I could think of only one place that would still be preparing my favorite meal. The Saratoga Diner was right down the road and served breakfast anytime. With only one other car in the lot, this would be a quick stop before hitting the road back to Vermont. Our waitress sat us across the room from the other two customers in the joint, Jeff Beck and his road manager! Missed opportunities? Not this time.

Jeff Beck signed his page, "I was not there." He inscribed with only a brief explanation. Exhausted and realizing that Beck was too, I never asked why.

We sent our niece a print of the photo we had taken as she posed backstage. Cat was overwhelmed by the excitement but, at nine, knew little of the artist. But the following week, when it was back to school and time for "What I did on my summer vacation," Cat brought her story and photo to class. While the reaction by her 4th grade classmates was muted, her teacher went bonkers. He was one of her favorite artists. "I'm so jealous," she told my niece. And that was that, until two years later when this boy she really liked told her that his favorite recording artist was guess who. Mr. Santana had just released his smash single "Smooth" with Rob Thomas and a new genera-

tion found another's soul. It was deja vu. It was pay it forward. It was six degrees of separation. It was true love. It was time to pull out the photograph, again.

Woodstock lives.

chapter two
PAUL NEWMAN & PHINIUS T. BARNUM

I paid my own way through college. By the summer of 1969, with only my senior year remaining, finding a teaching position to help relieve the financial burden of undergraduate studies at one of Ohio's most expensive schools weighed heavy on my mind. How was I going to pay off that massive, four-year $11,000 student loan?

This was my third summer back home in Connecticut and the first since freshman year that didn't find me working the graveyard shift for the U.S. Postal Service. Boy, those were the days. Graveyard was the 4 am to 10 am satellite run, five days a week. To qualify, I had to pass both the written and practical exams for the safe handling and driver skills needed to sit behind the wheel of the "Big Rigs." For succeeding, I was issued an official document that looked strikingly similar to a police officers ID and a gold badge that looked strikingly similar to a policeman's badge. I was 19 years old. Well shit, you don't have to be a rocket surgeon to figure out what a 19 year old stud muffin, on summer break from Miami University, one of the great party schools of the 1960s, is going to do with "FBI" credentials! Having seen how the pros did it on TV, I immediately went shopping for a flip open wallet to match my blossoming 007 persona. Going pub hopping would never be the same. After years of waiting in line at New York City's most popular night spots, that year it was time to test the waters. The line for the Bitter End, in

Greenwich Village, N.Y., was half a block long; not uncommon for a Saturday night. The Nitty Gritty Dirt Band was appearing and I was pumped to get a good seat. With confidence in my stride, I approached the front of the line, flipped open my new wallet long enough for the bouncer to read the words " United States Government Official" and the shiny gold badge opposite it, and boldly requested two seats at the bar. "Come right in sir" he offered. Another club employee hastily removed two patrons from their places at the bar and "Voila", we were enjoying the show. It was not uncommon back then for the government to hire young officers, known as narcs, to pose as college students, get in with the in crowd and act as informants... perhaps I fit the profile. In all honesty, I only pulled that stunt a few times but it never failed.

By mid summer, I had begun hearing rumors about a concert being planned for up-state New York. Details were sketchy but names like Dylan, The Band and The Beatles were tossed into the mix. Still, I had to stay focused on the bigger picture. My girlfriend was pissed off at me, my football professor at Miami, one Bo Schembeckler, hated my hippie gymnast guts because I wore "fag" bellbottom pants and flowery shirts to a conservative mid-western school and my parents couldn't understand why their "handsome," clean cut son would want to grow his hair long. To add insult to injury, I grew a mustache.

My very progressive and understanding parents allowed me to convert the basement of our modest cape house into a psychedelic, black lit, day glow lunar landscape, complete with a LEM (Lunar Excursion Module) hung from the ceiling by threads so as to allow for lunar landing simulations. I even got to try my hand at growing my own pot plant. When it reached a height of three feet, Scooby – my nickname for Mom -- got nervous and it was time to harvest. The former setting of our extensive Lionel train set was mine for another summer at home as long as I agreed to get a job and help with expenses. I ended up at a meat processing and packing plant in downtown, the worst job I ever had.

While I was busy honing my grinding and blending skills in a concrete and steel railed bunker adjacent to the train station, just a few blocks away a little-known Bassick High Schooldrop out by the name of Paul Leka was busy making pop music history, following his 1967 bubble gum smash hit that went on to top the charts at #1 worldwide. Paul decided early on that school was getting in the way of his fascination with contemporary music. One or the other had to go. His Connecticut Recording Studio was located on the second floor of an obscure Main Street walk-up. It's entryway was devoid of signage; a silent buzzer, the only means of entry. A decade would pass before I would get to walk through that nondescript entrance.

I grew up in the city that the great showman, con-man and philanthropist P. T. Barnum called home and the legendary actor and humanitarian Paul Newman once labeled "The Armpit" of Connecticut. Sure, Bridgeport had its anomalies, it's issues, its mafia controlled mayor, but all that was innocently off my radar in the city's north end; the perfect place to grow up middle class. For nine years, including kindergarten, childhood consisted of walking four miles a day to and from Sheridan Elementary school on a route that was dotted with friends' and classmates' homes, past the woods on Wayne Street to Merritt Street and up the hill to Tessney Circle. Knowing that the shortest distance between two places was a straight line, I seldom varied my route and, like my older brother Allan, four years before me, developed a familiarity critical to fostering a sense of well being and neighborhood.

The movie theater (where I had my first date and kiss with Nancy Brown when I was in the third grade) was just down the block. We sat in the back row and made out, but not before I gave her a "glamorous", red patent leather pocketbook as an expression of my love. All marriage hopes were dashed when her parents moved away the following year. Gee, I wonder now if ,perhaps, I came on a little too strong to win over the folks! Twelve years later, I'm waiting in the gift wrapping line at the Trumbull Shopping Center and this drop dead gorgeous brunette, standing two spaces ahead turns to me and asks, " Is your name Ron?" Yes. "Ron Evans?" Yes.

"Did you go to Sheridan School?" Yees. "You lived on Peet Street, right?" Yeees. "You were my first date, in the third grade." By this time she had everyone else's rapt attention in a scene straight out of Hollywood. "I'm Nancy Brown and I still have the red patent leather pocketbook you gave me!" We offered each other an extemporaneous hug as the gift-wrapping line broke into spontaneous applause. It was a made for the movies moment.

The Class of 1962 was notably, the most precocious group of students that ever attended Sheridan Elementary with half the class going steady by the 7th grade. I began hosting co-ed parties in my basement science lab with cutting edge games like, Seven Minutes in Heaven, Doctor and, of course the one that started it all, Spin the Bottle. On rec night , however, it was all about the dancing. Friday was record hop night. Vincent Haggerty, Carl Antignani, Frank Auriemma and I would take turns hosting the event in the school's auditorium. When it came to Rock and Roll, Vinny was our Renaissance man: A tall Irish catholic with a D.A., tight pants, and dance moves that pre-dated Michael Jackson and John Travolta by more than a decade. With a collection of 45 rpm records numbering in the hundreds, we could always count on Vinny to have the latest Little Eva or Stevie Wonder release to help get our young juices flowing. Every new release seemed to bring with it a new dance craze. Who could forget The Twist, The Peppermint Twist, The Fish, The Swim, The Stroll, The Hitch Hike, The Mashed Potatoes, The Hully Gully, The Watusi, The Freddie, The Monkey or the good old fashioned Bop? The slow dances were reserved for the "serious" couples who were not afraid of a little P.D.A. (public display of affection). It was a scene straight out of American Bandstand but with the girls we knew since kindergarten. They would become our first loves.

The week leading up to Woodstock was a busy one for the hamburger business. On several occasions, I was approached by friends who were planning on going, to join them but in the end, thought it best to stay home and work. Besides, my parents, who were leaving on a Canadian vacation on August 10, weren't expected back until the 18th or so. Someone had to hold down the fort, meaning that having the house to myself for a week seemed like a better call than having to pay good money to join a raucous crowd in upstate New York.

It wasn't until the news reports started rolling in about the size of the crowd, the peace and harmony that overcame the adversity, the co-operation by all factions of authority and the fact that it had become a free event, that I began to regret my decision. Ron, you so blew it this time, I contemplated. The greatest recording artists of my generation, the poets and writers who penned the lyrics that spoke to the ills of American social injustice and misguided war - all in one place for a celebration of human freedom and unrestricted indulgence; and I stayed home. WTF. I tried not to dwell on the consequences. On the up side, I did have some dates I brought back to my parent-less abode. That too would end abruptly. Scooby and The Father rolled in around 4 in the afternoon on Monday, August 18th with tales from the road and stories about their time in Canada. Knowing how bummed out I was about missing Woodstock, Scoobs saved the best for last. "So Ron", she explained. "We were coming down the Northway from Montreal this morning and stopped for gas in Lake George. There were young people everywhere, among them a group of hippies in a white VW bus that had run out of gas. They had pushed it from the exit." One of the girls from the group asked my mom if she could help. Well, talk about serendipity. Young kids trying to get home to their folks after an historic weekend of partying? Mom was all over that. Dad lent a hand pushing the micro-bus up to the pumps. Mom shared my regret about having missed the concert, with the girl who solicited the assistance. While the parents and the hippies said their goodbyes, the girl from the van disappeared briefly, then chased down my departing parents with a gift of thanks, acquired back stage that morning. The "pay it forward" contagion and ex-change, would take me on the journey of a lifetime.

Sheridan Elementary School,
Bridgeport, Connecticut.
Allan Evans photo, 2014

The class of '62 celebrates
classmate Grace Conigliaro's
birthday, 1953.
Courtesy of Grace Conigliaro Cribbins

Graduation day. Our dance idol
Vincent Haggerty is second
from right.
Courtesy of Grace Conigliaro Cribbins

The coolest house in the world to grow
up in — 50 Peet St.

Right: the famous floating kitchen table
designed by my dad in 1963.

chapter three
KENT STATE & "MOTHER" MIAMI

With only a few weeks left before returning to Oxford for senior year, and the summer coming to a close, there would not be enough time to complete the restoration on the first car I ever owned. When most of my classmates in high school were buying muscle cars or European sports car, I favored something with a little more history, a little more intrigue. On prom night, 1966, at Central High School in Bridgeport, Connecticut, only one car in the lot had a roll and pleated, burgundy mohair sofa for a back seat, complete with fringed curtains, built-in corner flower vases and an added mini-bar to complete the bedroom on wheels motif. True, I couldn't beat a single muscle car off the line, zero to sixty... nor could I cruise the strip with the top down but when it came to real estate for making out, the 1923 Buick, seven passenger semi-limousine may have held the Guinness record. This baby had 47-inch wheels and stood a dominant seven feet tall. With that much "pussy wagon" parked in the lot, I didn't even have to start the engine!

I found a rental unit for the Buick as the summer of Wood-stock drew to a close. My friend Andy's landlord, Mr. Center, wanted $9.00 a month. It was a single bay of a four car garage located behind his three family home off Capital Ave. Andy's mom, Betty, who lived on the second floor, would be around to keep an eye on it while I was at college; an easy task since I had already started the restoration and most of the car was in paper bags marked for identity and re-assembly. The body, the chassis and all those bags went into stingy Mr. Center's garage and I headed back to Miami, to finish up my B.S. in Physical Education, as the turbulent 60's drew to a close.

By the fall of '69, the war in Vietnam had claimed nearly 10,000 young lives. Our campus and that of our sister college, Kent State, had become key battlegrounds in the effort by the student body to move president Nixon and the congress toward withdrawal and the war's end. Nixon had campaigned the previous year under the guise of ending the war and bringing the troops home. He was hoping that the up-coming Draft Lottery would take the wind out of the Peace Movement by leveling the playing field and the degree of inclusion on the part of what he perceived as the privileged academic engine behind the dissent. Tension was high around the prag-matically nurturing Oxford, Ohio campus, known to students and alums as "Mother Miami" for that very reason. Founded in 1809 by an act of congress passed due to President George Washington's determination, Miami's 18,000 acres of farm land in the southwest corner of the state, was by 1969, one of the most beautiful all Greek revival, William and Mary-esque schools in the nation, with standards so respected it was, alike, referred to, in academic circles as Ohio's " Non-Ivy, Ivy! " This year there were a lot of unanswered questions swirling around "Campi." How would Miami's football team do in the Mid-American Conference this season with the absence of it's famous coach, Bo Schembeckler? Was it true that Simon and Garfunkel, the most respected poet and song writing duet perhaps in the world, were coming to Miami for the kickoff of their Campus Tour schedule? Was the Armed Services Committee of the U.S. government really going to hold the first Draft Lottery since World War II? It was impossible to stay focused on business as usual. The best educators seized the moment to teach the lessons of Civil Disobedience to a student body yearning to implement them. Their classes were overflowing beyond capacity. Philosophers like Professor John Weigel and Milton White of the Department of English in Upham Hall acquired rock star status with a protégé following to match. Having collaborated with writers including Ken Kesey, author of "The Electric Kool-aid Acid Test," and Rod Serling, creator of the TV series "Twilight Zone," provided Milton and John with experience that Miami's future poets and authors couldn't get enough of. What they built was a cult-like following of insiders known as the Miltonians and Weigelites. While many students opted to participate in anti-war protest events and meet-ups in leu of senior year electives, a bye in English Lit was not cool. Self-expression had become the new mantra of a generation. The principles which govern those free-doms were about to be put to the test.

Rallies on campus grew in attendance and frequency after Homecoming Week. The Lemon Pipers, known to the world for their bubble gum hit song, "Green Tambourine," but known around Miami's campus as the heavy acid rock band that performed uptown and down the alley in Mac n' Joe's Bar, kept us entertained and wanting to go higher on weekends. If you partied long enough and late enough, the payoff was fresh pastry and donuts at Beasley's Bakery up on High Street (get the double entendre). The bakers would arrive at about 2am to prepare that days good-ies and if the munchies struck, a rap on the back door got you a fresh, right out of the oven, donut. For a Miamian, that was the closest thing to a "Toasted Roll" you were ever going to find off campus in Oxford.

Most of the anti-war protests were held at or near the old campus center. Up-ham Hall's north stairway formed a natural stage and focal point for touring guest speakers and local organizers. For flyer distribution and student participation, Slant Walk, the main diagonal walkway between campus and uptown offered the most exposure. By mid October it was clear that two pivotal events were to take place before the holiday break that would impact virtually every student, teacher and res-ident of our tiny Ohio hamlet. The Republican controlled executive branch of the Armed Services had succeeded at implementing the Draft Lottery. It was scheduled for December 1st and would be broadcast live on national TV. More than a million young Americans' lives hung in the balance (an estimated 3.4 million service members were deployed in Vietnam during the conflict). The second event would help mitigate the first. Simon and Garfunkle were in fact coming to Miami and would be performing at Millett Hall on November 9th. The performance would be filmed for their TV special "Songs of America." I wasn't going to make the same mistake twice. I would not be staying home this time.

The gifted duo from New York drew the largest crowd Millett had ever seen and history would be made when at the start of the fifth song, Paul approached the microphone and told us that Art was about to perform this next song for the first time ever before a live audience. Paul walked into the dimmed light of stage rear and took a seat at the Baby Grand. Art stepped into the spotlight center-stage. Twelve thousand people were in hushed silence as the piano intro began. "When you're weary, feel small. When tears are in your eyes, I will dry them all." Is there anyone on the planet that does not know" Bridge Over Troubled Water?" How it builds so methodically and showcases Art Garfunkel's rapturing falsetto voice in a crescendo that, on that historic night, began the longest standing ovation I'd ever witnessed. It took the artists ten minutes to continue the concert. The rush would have to stay with us all school year as the troubled waters, politically, morally and socially, were just beginning to flow.

The word among those closest to the protest had it that if you were within the first 150 lottery numbers drawn, the odds were pretty good that you would be called up for duty. The next 50 to 75 would be stuck in purgatory and if you got lucky and drew a number higher than 225, you probably weren't going. In the same way I believe that only psychologically weak people need guns as a false sense of protection, I too believe that it takes more strength of character and moral fortitude to stand against any and all injustice in a peaceful manner, than it does to follow, blindly, a delusional theistic or philosophical imperative that is rooted in ignorance.

Knowledge is the most powerful weapon you will ever possess. Our father taught his three sons the lessons of war, at an early age. "Peace," he said, "takes more guts and is much harder to achieve. If your number comes up, I would rather leave the country than loose one of my sons to that senseless war." Dad, who never made it through high school, spent the rest of his life catching up. With an acutely heretic sense of self ambition and the "chutzba" to try anything at least once, Sydney (Eckstein) Evans had me flying his Piper Cub airplane, acquired when he moved to Bridgeport, by the time I was 6. Simply flying would not have been sufficient for this former WWII Air force bomber technician. We had to take it to the next level...call it the X-Games of private piloting if you like. I called it the most fun you could have at 4,000 feet. Who, in his right mind, stunt pilots a Piper Cub? Answer; someone with bigger balls than you or I, who had once flown with the famous Wiley Post and had personally interviewed Chuck Yeager, that's who. So, if you want to do a Death Spiral or an Inside Loop, I'm your man. Father, I thank you for the life lessons.

On the afternoon of December 2nd, Alexander Pirnie, Republican from New York, drew the first of 365 numbered balls to determine the draft status and individual fate of every young American male. For a generation that had never lived with war until Vietnam but had prepared for atomic annihilation, the whole idea of leaving such a principled decision to the luck of the draw seemed absurd. Yet, however absurd, there we were, like subjects in a slave auction, awaiting our fate at the behest of an ever-growing Industrial/Military enterprise empowered by government, but driven by a war-for-profit corporate obsession. Who would be "the first one on the block to have their kid come home in a box!" Country Joe McDonald had famously chanted at Woodstock just months before. Lucky # 1 was September 14th. The fraternity brothers at Sigma Nu on Tallawanda heard the scream from across the street. A third story window opened up at Swing Hall dormitory there and the sounds of silence were shattered by the impact of the cathode ray TV screen exploding on contact as it hit the ground below. Miami had its first victim. Many more would follow, but for now anyway, my parents would not be moving to Canada and I would not be deciding between two cold climates; our neighbors to the north or a jail cell here. My birth date drew #343.

December break couldn't happen soon enough. The Nixon administration had gotten itself into a quagmire over how to draw down the Vietnam War, which had become so unpopular at home, while seemingly attempting a diplomatic peace treaty with the North Vietnamese government in Paris. Negotiations were falling apart as Miami students headed home for the holidays.

In 1969, there were three major television networks; CBS, NBC and ABC. The competition for coverage, including first-ever live coverage, of the Vietnam war was as omnipotent as the conflict itself. Day after day, month after month reporters on the front lines would send back live satellite images of America's young men taking heavy fire or suffering more casualties from the napalm inferno or agent orange de-foliating poison used by our own government. Massacres became monthly events as Cambodia and Laos were brought into the confluence. Conveyor belts lined with body-bags were the psychotic consequence of an Executive Branch and Military out of control. The shear insanity of it all just couldn't continue. Something had to give and in the spring of 1970, Miami University and its sister college Kent State, were ground zero. The messengers of my generation were the song writers and counter-culture artists whose words meant so much more than their showmanship or panache. It was the dichotomy between the self-evident truth that all people were endowed with inalienable right to pursue life, liberty and happiness versus the message we were being fed everyday that communism was the evil monster waiting to take over the world and America's military power was the only hope for freedom. I have always and continue to adopt George McGovern's motto, " I'm tired of old men dreaming up wars for young men to die in." We'll come back to said premise later.

Meanwhile, some artists couldn't satiate their appetite for freedom by song alone. Janis Joplin had secured her legacy at Woodstock but I wouldn't catch up to her until February 22nd, 1970 at Clark University in Wooster, Massachusetts. The intimate, on campus, venue where she "performed" and Big Brother propped her up, was to be among her last east coast concerts. My Trumbull High friend Mike Dworkin invited me to his school to see the show which featured a very intoxicated Ms. Joplin stumbling around the stage intermittently, when, in fact, she chose to occupy the stage . Being that I too was somewhat (ok, very) wrecked that night, the only thing I can tell you with "certainty" is, I slept with Janis and woke up the next day without my mustache. Seriously, the really cool thing was, when my parents picked me up at Kennedy Airport a few days later, neither of them noticed that the much belied lip hair had vanished. I finally brought it to their attention somewhere around exit 5 of the Connecticut Turnpike in Stamford, Connecticut. You could almost anticipate the response. "We knew there was something different, we just didn't quite know what it was." I started singing a few verses from "Hair" and they finally got it.

Winter break was over by March but Richard Nixon's secret diplomatic agenda to invade formerly neutral Cambodia was being leaked to the press and on to protest organizers around the country. At Miami, it was time to take action. The ROTC building, located across the street from the student center would be the obvious target of contempt for the accelerating war effort. Anti-war sentiment had reached such a pitch that many recruits themselves began joining the student protests. Several hundred students invaded the Reserve Officers Training Center in later April and in days the facility was essentially shut down and occupied. Negotiations between school president Dr. Philip Shriver and Ohio's governor Rhodes stalled as National Guard troops were deployed at Kent State and just off campus at Miami. Bucolic Oxford had become an armed camp. Students lined High Street as troops, brandishing loaded rifles and tear-gas canisters, taunted peaceful students and encroached onto private property. Just days before the Kent State massacre, I recall witnessing the Ohio State police marching up High Street hill toward town as sign-carrying students, incensed by their presence, lined the street in peaceful protest. K-9 assisted soldiers patrolled the adjoining sidewalks. Suddenly there were words exchanged with Beta Theta Pi fraternity, diagonally across from the entrance to Slant Walk, on the north side of the street and in an instant, dogs and troops rushed into the house as tear-gas was released and fraternity brothers were clubbed in their own rooms. I ran to relieve the ocular pain, but the pain that would not subside was purely psychological. How could MY country turn so hostile toward it's own people?

The students who were assassinated by a group of 19 guardsmen on Kent's campus on May 4th were not even within striking distance of them. Most were 50 to 200 yards away and all were unarmed, when they were shot dead. Miami and Kent were closed for weeks as university administrators tried to regroup and the nation mourned. On May 21st, just two weeks later, David Crosby, Steven Stills, Graham Nash and Neil Young met at The Record Plant Recording Studio in Los Angeles and in one session, recorded both Young's "Ohio" and Stills' "Find the Cost of Freedom" for immediate release:

"Find the cost of freedom, buried in the ground
Mother earth will swallow you, lay your body down."
—Stephen Stills, 1970 (Goldhill Music)

If one delves deeply enough into historic documents and time lines, assuaging a thirst for the truth, the reward can be profound, the consequences benevolent. Such is the case here, with consequences that have literally affected every U.S. citizen since Woodstock.

Immediately following the Kent State massacre, Patrick Ducey, a freshman student senate candidate at Miami and member of the national peace protest organization, The Student Mobilization Committee, flew to Boston to participate in a northeastern regional steering committee meeting. Shortly after the meeting got underway, a gang of thugs brandishing blackjacks and pin laden grips, broke into the hall and severely beat several of the attendees. The perpetrators turned out to be from the militant wing of the Students for a Democratic Society, (The SDS). Their objective; to shut down the peace movement in America and falsely re-brand the pacifists as militant troublemakers. The conservative republican base took the bait. Back in Oxford, Miami's V.P. for Development, one John Dolibois, proceeded to use his unbridled small town power to paint the anti-war protestors as hoodlums and unpatriotic losers who should be expelled. Dolibois went one step further, suggesting that professors who sympathized with the hippies should be fired, among them my own uncle Professor Milton White. Who were some of these militant outcasts from the formerly peaceful SDS movement, hoping to put an end to John Lennon's Imagine? Their names would remain obscure for two decades until the privileged son of the former United States president, George H.W. Bush, who, along with the First Lady, Barbara, questioned not only his ability to lead a nation but perhaps his ability to remain sober, would too, be shocked by his victory in 2000. W.'s conspiratorial theft of the presidency shocked the hell out of everyone except the handful of thugs who masterminded his campaign and, in so doing, fortuitously stole the nations eupraxophy. As Americas youth prepared to celebrate peace & music on Yasgurs Farm, Geoge W. Bush' future brain trust were busy orchestrating the military style dismemberment of the Peace Movement. The malfeasance and utter distortion of reality that the likes of Richard Perle, Paul Wolfowitz, Bill Kristol and Donald Rumsfeld among the neo-conservative dictators behind George W. Bush's ascent to the White House, would inflict on America, will take decades to obfuscate. In a plutocracy, it's always the few that spoil it for the many and these guys were masters at the deception.

Clockwise from top - My first car. The 1923 Buick seven passenger

"Pussy Wagon" sedan used in the filming of the movie Ghost Story (1981).

Mac & Joe's Bar — Oxford, Ohio — Stoner home of the Lemon Pipers.

Slant Walk gates of Miami University, site of my first tear gassing during the anti-Vietnam war protests.

Millett Hall - Home of Simon & Garfunkel's debut performance of "Bridge Over Troubled Waters", *

Professor and author Milton White relaxing at home in his living room at 325 E. Vine St., Oxford, Ohio.

One of two fraternity houses on High Street attacked by police on April 15 & 16, 1970. The coalition of fraternities were Zeta Beta Tau, Phi Gamma Delta and Beta Theta Pi. The Ohio State Police used tear gas, K-9 police dogs and clubs on innocent students.

chapter four
"PRIDE IN OUR PAST"

An anti-climactic senior graduation took place at Miami in early summer that year and I was off to the next big thing; finding a teaching job in my major course of study, Physical Education.

Armed with the credentials, and the Bo Schembeckler football legacy, a summer full of interviews could not land me a single job offer in P.E. I simply didn't look like a Jock. It was time to bring in the heavy hitters. My agent got me an interview in Trumbull, Connecticut for a shop teacher position that was in urgent need of filling, just days before the school year was to begin. I would have to work under a T.E.P. (temporary emergency permit) but because Trumbull was just north of Bridgeport, I could live at home one more year and save the money I would need to get a place on my own. The " Den of Sin " downstairs, was still available, I was told. It's time to get a haircut and help change the world; teacher orientation is in one week.

Hillcrest Jr. High was not your run of the mill intermediate public school facility. Trumbull's upscale, mostly white, suburban rural neighborhoods of 1/2 and 1 acre minimum estates, was home to arguably the most advanced, public school facility in the nation, including an Olympic swimming pool, a two story glass atrium library, full-sized gymnasium with bleachers, a state of the art theater/ auditorium And get this, it's own fully operational Planetarium.

Opportunity for creative teaching abounded; Carpe Diem, the young faculty's mantra. I seized the moment with vigor, as John F. Kennedy had taught me, years before.

I may have been hired to teach metal shop, but my formal and less formal studies were in Geology, Power Transmission, Astronomy, Quantum Physics, Relativity and Ecology. It didn't take long for Roger, one of the new science teachers, and me to begin hatching a plan to direct some of that young energy into one of the most necessary and timely environmental issue solutions of the day, recycling. What was not to love about teaching these eager, fresh minds how to save the planet and make money for the common good, all while learning a life lesson about making a difference in your community and beyond. So off we went to create the Great Society. We called it The Hillcrest Jr. High Ecology Club and it took off like a greyhound. One month after its, administration approved, first after school meeting, two dozen students were enthusiastically on board. Members took the lessons of recycling home to their families and before you could say Poly Vinyl Chloride, students began arriving at school with more than books. Car trunks full of sorted paper, cardboard, and plastic overwhelmed the schools dumpsters. By Thanksgiving, the experiment had reached such a level of participation that, to meet the demand, we had to seek help from a trucking firm willing to drop off an 18 wheel, full size trailer and pick it up a week later for recycling. The Ecology Club of Trumbull's Hillcrest Jr. High had struck a nerve. The local radio and TV stations soon got wind of the youth led initiative and by "Christmas" vacation, Roger, myself and the student club officers were fielding almost daily interviews and weekly speaking engagements. Our school was the talk of the state. It was all good, or so we thought.

Shortly after New Years, which was celebrated in Trumbull with an abundance of private, A-list house parties, I received a call from the president of the local Lions Club, asking if I would come to one of their members only meetings and give a talk about The Ecology Club at school. I, of course, accepted with pleasure. Growing up, wasn't it always the service groups that you were told did such great things for people in need around the country. So, off I went to the late afternoon gathering of the Trumbull Lions; "Bite'em, Bite'em, Bite'em!"

The first order of business, before the official business: Have a drink. The second order of business; have another drink. I graciously declined. By the time they got done chanting and singing sophomoric lion themed verses, half of the attendees were in the bag. I followed along curiously. Next up, the pledge of allegiance, the national anthem and finally the benediction. I stood up, at attention, for the pledge, but since I didn't believe that the words, " One nation, under god, with liberty and justice for all," were true, I did not recite them and would not, in practice, put my hand over my heart. Only one Lion seemed to notice and my speech was well received.. I was thanked and given an official desktop lion statue for my efforts. I'm thinking, you probably have an idea where this is going. A week later, I am summoned to the principal's office, to answer allegations that I am Un-American and perhaps an inappropriate role model for Trumbull's youth. Principal D'Matto tells me that one of the members of the Lions has filed a formal complaint with the board of education. Mr. Evans, I am told, showed callous disregard for his patriotic duty by refusing to say the pledge or salute the flag. "They want you fired, Ron, and working here on a T.E.P. diminishes your job security." I enlisted the help of the Connecticut National Education Association and when the whole controversy went public, I was branded the "No Pledge Teacher." All this, over a seemingly innocuous event that didn't even take place at an official school sanctioned gathering? It didn't add up, Why such a vicious attack on a respected and successful young instructor? I tried to recount the brief yet sometimes lurid events that took place in and out of school during the previous months. Maybe I was missing something. I recalled being invited to the superintendent's home during the holidays, months earlier, where Mrs. Superintendent, a hot little blonde trophy, cornered me upstairs for an extemporaneous petting session. I was, after all, the new, single and apparently upwardly vertical conquest in the world of the Desperate Housewives. Even if I wasn't the predator here, I calculated, I was going down. That had to be it.

The N.E.A. lost the case. It was never about the merits or the abrogation of my Constitutional rights. It never got that far. It came down to my lack of procedural rights under the temporary emergency permit and in the end I had to acknowledge that it would not be in my, or my students', best interest to fight City Hall. I finished out the school year a hero in the eyes of some, a villain in the eyes of others and a victim in my own. Either way, I could accept the lesson taught and vowed, as always, not to shy away from challenges to my core principles and personal freedoms. Time to move on. A summer of job interviews ended in disappointment once again, but now, I had an agent who had the inside track on an opening in Stamford for a middle school graphics art instructor position that remained vacant even after the school year began. I qualified, having both a B.S. in Education and a pulse. No time to prepare; it was already October. I was just getting adjusted to my new digs, when a phone call from a former Trumbull colleague would resurrect old wounds and open new ones. The illusive answer I had been hoping for was finally revealed. Turns out, the No Pledge Teacher fiasco was just a smoke screen to conceal the much more clandestine and financially corrupt issue that belied the Town's most respected selectman and the land that was leased back as a landfill. Seems that the Hillcrest Ecology Club's recycling campaign was so successful that the renewal of the landfill lease had been placed in jeopardy because there wasn't enough garbage to justify the additional space. One Town official, I am told, who also happened to own the

land leased to the landfill, chose personal gain over moral, ethical and community benevolence. I was just collateral damage. Gives a whole new meaning to Trumbull's official Motto: "Pride in our past, Faith in our Future."

Photo by Allan Evans

chapter five
THE REAL DORAL COUNTRY CLUB

Following in the footsteps of artists like the legendary story teller Harry Chapin and Connecticut's own Simms Brothers, (who would go on to record with Madonna, David Bowie, Billie Joel, Carly Simmon and many more) I will count among my memories, meeting Paul Leka and having him proudly show off the (green) tambourine hanging on the wall behind his desk. The #1 Mega hit that propelled Connecticut Recording Studio into rock history was recorded right on this very spot, by non other than the Lemon Pipers from Oxford, Ohio, home of Miami University. It's the new 4.5 degrees of separation and the song, if you haven't guessed by now, was "Green Tambourine." We were there as guests of our dear friend and next door neighbor, Frank Simms who, along with his brother George, were adding the background vocals for a new Harry Chapin album to be called" Verities and Balderdash." The cut they were working on this night was the single cover from the album that Harry's wife Sandy had written after the birth of their son Josh. We took our places next to Paul at the mixer board ...Frank and George at the studio microphones. Paul cued up the lead vocals which remained almost ghosted in the background while the Simmses oohed and aahed their Everly Brothers inspired harmony clearly and markedly in the foreground. "A child was born just the other day, he came to the world in the usual way." "Cats in the Cradle" holds a very special place for me, not just because I was there to see its creation, but perhaps more importantly because Frank and his wife Terry and Linda and I were together, driving back from dinner in their green VW micro-bus when it played on the New York City radio stations for the first time. We pulled off the road and cranked up the volume, savoring the moment with every verse. We cheered and cried. I questioned the apparent loss of the background that seemed so loud in the studio; I was so naive, but it really didn't matter anyway. The moment was both innocent and the end of innocence. I knew right then that Frank was destined to follow the footsteps of his father Frank Sr. and uncle Hank.

Back in the 1950's and 60's, Frank Sr. was the famous announcer for such classic TV shows as I Love Lucy, Merv Griffin, Candid Camera and Lassie. His brother Hank (Uncle Hank as we knew him) went on to become one of the most famous television announcers in history. As the voice of Quinn Martin productions, he came into the living rooms of millions of Americans every week as the announcer for The F.B.I., Barnaby Jones, The Dating Game and The Fugitive. So, I guess it should come as no surprise to find out, all these years later, that the guy who sat next to us, guitar in hand, in the garden at the Waveny Castle in New Canaan, Connecticut on June 24th, 1973 as we took our wedding vows, was poised to carry on a family voice-over and announcer legacy well into the new millennium.

You'll recognize Frank's now famous voice as that of the Kool-Aid Man, the Honeycomb Cereal mascot or the Geico ringtone. He appears frequently on Saturday Night Live and recorded the theme song for their TV Funhouse segment. He won an Emmy in 2007 for his performance of the song "Q without U," from the PBS children's series, Between the Lions. But for Linda and me, he will always be our backdoor neighbor on Doral Farm, the original 60 acre estate built by the Dodge motor car family in Stamford, where innocence and dreams converged; and for a brief moment, Rolling Stone and Rock Scene magazines took notice.

In the fall of 1973, shortly after Linda and I returned from our hippie van cross country honeymoon, Blue Sky Records producer Steve Paul rented the main estate house on Doral and threw what was later reported in the Rock world as "The" party of the year. "Everyone who could possibly attend made sure to be on hand for the event. Paul provided a lavish repast that included lemon/lime chicken, wine & apricot macaroon mousse – all served in attractive picnique baskets lined with blue (sky) tinfoil," recalls blonde beauty Bebe Buell, Todd Rundgren's date (and later, Liv Tyler's mom) with whom Linda and I shared the estate master bedroom that night.

Doral Farm, so renamed after the founders of the empire, Doris and Al (as in, Dor-al) Kaskel purchased the breathtaking oasis from the Dodge family and years later, placed its care and management with a New York City firm responsible for leasing the several cottages and guest houses scattered about the 6,000 square foot Dutch Colonial Estate House and British Lake country style, Main Street epicenter. Linda and I rented the quaint, gambrel roofed, Gardeners cottage across from the white tiled breeding barn. Frank and Terry Simms were maybe 20 feet away, in the Herdsman's Cottage. The Estate House had been vacant for years. Mr. Antie, the property manager, lived in the former chicken coop, across the road and up the hill and tended to mind his own business. So there we were, Frank, Terry, Linda and I virtually alone on 60 of the most picturesque, rolling, lush and undisturbed acres of New England farm land imaginable. Life on Doral was rich with baby fox growing up in the field behind the sun porch, Canada geese swimming in the lake central to the lower 40 and "Rita" the polo pony grazing along the white rail fence. Most dramatic and proximal to downtown Stamford was Doral's tranquil silence and peaceful allure; that is, until Frank began practicing his electric guitar riffs, right out back. Frank's practice room was a 10 x 10 box, facing the "Stalk" field. To achieve the sound quality desired, he had hung moving blankets acquired from his part time mover's job, on all four walls. It wasn't pretty, but it did the job and as the school year progressed for Linda and me, so did Frank's musicianship.

On June 24th, 1973, Frank sat garden stage left before an intimate crowd of about 125 as Linda and I said "we do". The day's rain had given way to brilliant sun and late afternoon passing fair weather clouds in the lush walled formal garden so reminiscent of Love Story. Waveny Castle, the English Tudor estate home of the late founder of the Texaco Oil Company in nearby New Canaan, had not yet been discovered by Martha Stewart, as one of her top ten picks for best places to get married, so, when in '72, we began planning our day, we were able to rent the entire estate, with a little help from our friends, for the absurd rate of two hundred and fifty bucks. An afternoon of planting and painting in the garden, which hadn't seen use in a while, and we were ready for Frank's debut and our big day. We entered the ceremony to Frank's rendition of "Today", by Jefferson Airplane, and Crescendo-ed, just before our vows, to "Color My World", by Chicago and finally, "A Whiter Shade of Pale," by Procol Harem. As we said goodbye to our guests and hopped aboard our Honda CB 450 motorcycle to begin our married life together, we were unsuspecting of the many changes that would affect the dynamics of both personal and familial relationships for years to come. But, for right now, the only thing on our minds was, where the hell was the Chevy van that we had ordered, four months ago, as a wedding present for each other?

Every Hippie, even the employed ones, wanted a van. The allure was the utilitarian configuration of the vehicle, which gave it's user the option of transporting tools or equipment conveniently (as in amplifiers and instruments), or ease of conversion into a camper, while still benefiting from good gas mileage and maneuverability. It was your own little world on wheels. Lin and I had ours all picked out by February, four months before the wedding. We were pooling our savings to give each other the gift that would keep on giving. Some of Linda's contribution would come from the insurance reimbursement she had received as a result of her former house-mate sinking her gorgeous 1971 Fiat Spider roadster convertible in a lake, just months before the wedding. Don't ask. It took two wreckers and a rowboat to retrieve it, as a total loss. Linda recalls the fish still swimming inside the speedometer when she went to claim the remains.

Redman Chevrolet in Stamford had given us the best price and a guarantee that they could get our new van, with time to spare. It was being built, to our requirements, at the G.M. factory in Lordstown, Ohio. Our plan was to leave the wedding ceremony, in hippie van style, and head out for a five week cross country tour. All of the necessary amenities like curtains, rugs, porto-potty, and cook stove had already been acquired as the date drew closer. It was now May and Redman's General Manager was stuck on the reprise that the computers in Tarrytown, New York were still down, so he couldn't trace the whereabouts of the vehicle; "But, rest assured, we will have it for your wedding." Weeks became days and at this point we began hanging out at the dealership hoping that, if we made a nuisance of ourselves, they would understand that we were serious and get our van delivered. When that failed, we took over the manager's office and started addressing thank you cards for wedding guests. It was now less than a week to the big day and still no van. We thought of contacting the press and even picketing the dealership but, in the end, the motorcycle seemed like the easiest short term solution for the wedding. We would deal with Redman's afterward.

Two days after the wedding and still waiting to leave on our honeymoon, we had reached our wit's end with that Chevy dealer. My parents felt terrible for us and probably couldn't wait for our departure either, so, when we stopped by for a visit, my dad asked if we had tried calling General Motors directly. Well, I guess I always thought that common folk had to deal with the stores or dealerships. "How do we do that", I asked. "Do you have the VIN # of your van and the location of the factory?" he inquired. "Yes, the dealer had provided us with that information." I answered. He turned around, picked up the wall phone and called information. In less than 30 seconds, he had the 800 number for the G.M. plant in Ohio. "Hi, we are trying to locate a vehicle that is being built by your factory as a wedding present. Can you help us?" I listened on the extension as the factory expeditor told my father that the vehicle had been built back in March and was sitting out in the yard waiting to be put on a train for delivery. Man, was I pissed! We had been jerked around for months by Redman's and it was sitting there the whole time. We told the story to the expeditor and she said that she would leave a note on the bulletin board for the morning crew. It would be placed on TOMORROW'S train. She then gave us the name and number for the trucking company that would pick it up in Little Ferry, New Jersey and bring it to Redman's. They, in turn, put a memo on their bulletin board to off-load the van as soon as it arrived and deliver it directly to the dealer. After all the bull shit, we ended up doing the whole thing ourselves. What they couldn't do in 4 months, we had done ourselves, in less than 72 hours. It was a lesson I never forgot. Don't waste your time with the suits; if your needs are not being addressed, go right to the top.

She was a real beauty, burnt orange and white with a palomino interior. A 1973 Chevy, 3/4 ton long body, built to order for the purpose of conversion, at a later date, into an extended roof, high tech, luxury, hippie camper van (Self-delivered price, $3,755).

Neither were all hippies dirt-laddened dropouts. It took us all of one day to get our new "Honeymoon Home on Wheels," outfitted with the curtains, carpets, por-to-john and in-sundries, all previously acquired and needed to spend the better part of our summer vacation touring America. By the first of July, we were on the road and heading west.

Patricia Kiracofe photos

Top to bottom: Our gardeners cottage on Doral Farm. Frank and Terry Simms' house is barely visible behind left.

The Doral farm pond in 2013.

Our cottage living room 1972.

The newly weds return from their 5 week "Hippie van" cross country honeymoon, August 1973.

chapter six
DISCOVERING "NEW CONNECTICUT"

When Xerox Corporation broke ground for their new International headquarters at 800 Long Ridge Road in Stamford, Connecticut, Linda and I had already been living together for five years, two on Doral Farm and three renting next door to Jackie Robinson's son David and back to back with the Moochers of Roxbury Road. The announcement of the Xerox development sent real estate prices through the roof. Any chance of home ownership on two teachers' salaries, even on the gilded gold coast of the nation's wealthiest state, were ripped asunder. Stamford was quickly becoming a tax-friendly alternative for the Manhattan elite and their corporate weltanschauung. One of Linda's students, whose father had invented fiber optics at the RCA lab on High Ridge, once boasted that his middle school weekly allowance was probably more than she made teaching him. His failure was in not understanding that she was doing exactly what she wanted to do and her rewards were priceless. His privileged life was so empty, he became a kleptomaniac with a police record, just for cheap thrills. Don't envy the wealthy. If you must envy, envy those who have a passion for this life and a plan to make it better for everyone and everything in it. Make THEM your role models and participate in their efforts.

One of our fellow teachers had a summer place in East Wallingford, Vermont, on the way to Killington Ski area. Their son and daughter-in-law were selling an A-frame ski chalet just up the road in the state's highest town, Belmont. The Houstons knew that Lin and I ran the Cloonan Middle School Ski Club and that one of our favorite mountains was Okemo, virtually next door to Belmont. Elaine Houston suggested that we take the keys to the A-frame for a spring skiing weekend. Take it for a test drive, so to speak. Have fun. Oh, and don't forget to stop at the Belmont Store and get some dry aged steaks for dinner. HELLO! I think they already had the sales agreement drawn up before we left. In 1976, an uncleared acre of land in Stamford, Connecticut was selling for $34,000.00 or more. We inked the deal, in "New Connecticut," Vermont's original name, for the house, the acre, the well and the wood pile for a grand total of $7,700. If that wasn't utopian enough, farmers Ray and Claire, who owned the adjoining 750 acres of breathtaking Green Mountain National Forest, were happy to open up for us in advance of our arrival on weekends, anytime. It all sounded too good to be true. It was even better. Vermont's highest (in more ways than one) mountain village had, over the years, become a favorite getaway for members of Greenwich Village's "Little Red School House" movement and the post Woodstock Generation. Who knew? Moon-lit and star-clustered crystal clear nights over Star Lake cast a Truman Show - like sense of belonging and sharing in something meta-physical that the world outside just wasn't privy to. Growing and sharing your organic garden with neighbors. Pot luck dinners on the weekends. Afternoon volleyball out behind the old Parmeter house till dark. Awesome, local-vore weed!

By the following year, we knew that Vermont's Green Mountains were calling us and that we would have to listen. After 8 years of creative curriculum and challenging administrative direction, Cloonan Middle School was about to be taken over by a new regime, spearheaded by a rumored mafia affiliated principal with a "take no prisoners" attitude and an M.O. of climbing the ladder to Superintendent-hood. By advancing innuendo and intimidation prior to his scheduled take over in 1978, he pissed off so many faculty members that, by the end of the 1977 school year, an unprecedented 34 of the 69 teachers there told "Black Mike" to stick his agenda up his ass and they quit. I'm pleased to report that "Black Mike" never made it to his dreamed superintendent-ship along the Gilded Connecticut Coast, while 34 former great middle school teachers moved on, in pursuit of a personal definition for happiness. We said goodbye to Doral, bid our fellow teachers a passionate farewell, packed only our most treasured belongings and, possessing the strongest sense of personal freedom and adventure, headed for the Vermont hills.

Meanwhile, out in L.A., a young rock n' roll prodigy by the name of Phil "Floatin" Houghton, who, by the age of 16, became the first white musician to tour with an all black rock group (you may have heard of them, they were called "The Jackson Five") was planning a personal life-changing adventure of his own. Phil had grown up in privilege. His family's friends' Beverly Hills neighbors were, on one side, the Crosbys, as in Bing, and on the other side, literally and figuratively, the Reagans, as in Ronald and Nancy. By the summer of 1978, Phil and his wife D'Anne had shut down and sold off the bulk of the assets associated with "La Chateau" Recording Studio, L.A.'s first 42 track facility which his dad helped him finance a couple of years before. Designed and custom built by Frank Fisher, the patriarch of the Fisher Audio empire, La Chateau was state of the art. To guarantee perfect sound reproduction and replication, Phil had two matching sets of monitors built by Fisher, one for the studio mixing board and one for tape and record home listening. After several years of hosting recording sessions with some of the most celebrated Jazz and R&B musical talents, La Chateau had become a liability and a source of personal fear for Phil. Lost sleep and a loaded gun under the pillow was no way to raise a family.

Autumn came early to the Vermont hillside hamlet of Belmont. Farmer Ray stopped by our A-frame on Straight Road to both teach a city slicker how to fell a tree with more than a boy scout hatchet and to let us know that a new young couple had come to town. "Why don't you come to the co-op meeting tonight? I'll introduce you to the folks who bought the Parmeter House. They just moved here from California and I think you guys will hit it off." Well it was love at first organic produce order. Phil had all the panache of a rock star in exile, accompanied by his drop dead gorgeous blonde, valley girl wife. We swapped stories of the counter-culture, national and world politics, the meaning of life and of course, rock and roll. By the end of the meeting, we not only had a new source for locally grown vegetables, but the makings of a long term friendship with the Houghtons. Phil and D'Anne had purchased the palatial, 5,000 sq. ft. Parmeter House, right smack in the center of town, fully furnished with 19th century oak and rosewood antiques, with only one stipulation: the 25 X30 living room with 12 foot high ceilings be completely emptied out so that Phil's prized La Chateau Recording Studio monitor could be installed.

Do you remember the famous Memorex Commercial where the guy sits down in his lounge chair, flips on his Memorex Tape Recorder and experiences sound so pure and loud that it blows his hair and body back with such intensity that he almost falls back off his chair? One plush antique lounge chair sat strategically located midway between the two 800 watt, five foot tall, two hundred pound John B. Lansing hand built speaker cabinets powered by a Phase Linear 4000 Amplifier. After a few hits on some homegrown weed, it was time for my initiation. Phil chose to spin vinyl for the most intense and realistic sound reproduction. He cued up an Aierto cut called "Chicks in their Shells." Sixty seconds later, my life had changed forever! To this day I am yet to hear anything, short of a live concert, that comes close to the purity and un-destorted realism of the "La Chateau" system.

Life in the mountains was moving at both a snails pace, seemingly light years away from the burning issues of the day, and simultaneously post hast and beyond our control. Linda and I had become so close with Phil and D'Anne that when, in the summer of '79, they made preparations for the home birth of their second child, they asked us to play a most intimate, emotional and participatory role. We had already disclosed to them that children were not a fit for our life's ambitions. We were child free by choice, but D'Anne was about to teach us a few new life lessons.. Phil's sound room was converted to "Abbey's Birth Place." D'Anne made it look easy. A few hours' labor, followed by a front load washer discharge, 45 minutes of contractions and "Viola", daughter #2 named for the Beatles Album and address of the famed London recording studio. To this day, when asked who she saw first at birth, Abbey proudly discloses that it had to be the guy holding the camera and microphone less then 3 feet from mothers labia. This was Phil and D'Anne's greatest gift of extended love and shared physiology. If you've been there, you know. We laughed, we cried, we kissed, we partied; we all collapsed in complete exhaustion.

Abbey was still breast feeding when Ronald Reagan's campaign to capture the White House started taking on the moniker of a legitimate contender. Phil was getting concerned. He and the Reagan kids used to play together and in moments of innocence Phil got to see the inner most personal dynamics the Reagan's private life. It was not pretty. He would talk about how Nancy drank and was often unable to function as a responsible mother, but of deeper insight, were his recollections of Ronald. Ron and Patti's father was never there for them when they needed him the most, Phil explained. "He was a terrible father," he continued. And when he was there, he was incapable of relating to the needs of his kids. Driven by his conservative political aspirations and buttressed by Hollywood one liners, he was "a dangerous man," Phil said."The things I heard that guy say and the chauvinistic, bigoted and homophobic comments he would come out with in front of his children were scary."

As we sat out behind Phil and D'Anne's Parmeter Victorian house overlooking Star Lake under the late summer, moon-lit, Vermont evening sky, Phil was already planning his expatriation. "If that guy gets the Presidency, he will destroy this country," Phil insisted. I remember him saying something like, "He can read lines to a monkey but he's clueless about almost everything else."

On November 7th, 1980 the unimaginable happened to Phil; his friends' lunatic neighbor became the President of the United States. Within weeks, Floatin' Houghton packed a few belongings, said good-bye to his life in America and hopped a plane for Fiji Island, never to return. The last time I spoke with Phil was in 2011 when his daughter Abbey, who had come to visit Linda and me at the place of her birth, called him at his recently acquired New Zealand home and recording studio. He had remarried and raised a family in the land he always knew was more open, creative, secular and free than that of a post-Reagan presidency and as the years passed, although rightfully guilty of being compulsive himself, Phil proved an accurate prognosticator.

Let's take a quick look at the historical record of our Neo-con superhero, Mr. Ronald Reagan:

- As governor of California, he signed into law the largest tax increase in the history of any state.

- As President, Reagan raised taxes in seven of his eight years in office, including 4 times in just two years, after campaigning as an anti tax candidate. Reagan the anti-tax zealot is simply myth.

- During his term in office, Reagan nearly tripled the federal deficit to 3 trillion dollars. By enacting major tax cuts during his first year in office, especially for his large corporate donors, government revenues plummeted. The conservative delusion that some how tax cuts create more revenue sank our treasury deeper and deeper in debt; a debt that he failed miserably, even after increases in gasoline and business taxes, to recover from.

- Reagan's 1981 tax cuts shot the un-employment rate to almost 11 percent while the top corporate wage earners tripled and quadrupled their profits.

- Although he promised to "Move boldly, decisively and quickly to control the runaway growth of federal spending," federal spending in fact ballooned under his Presidency after adding the Department of Veterans Affairs with a budget of over 100 billion dollars and a payroll of 300,0000 people.

- As governor of California in 1967 Reagan signed into law a bill to liberalize that state's abortion laws to give women there the right to choose. As president, he advocated for prohibition of all abortion, except to save the mother's life.

But, these facts pale in comparison to Ronald Reagan's 3 most egregious failings:

1. Reagan illegally funneled weapons to Iran when the U.S. Congress had an embargo against it, then used some of the funds to arm the Nicaraguan rebels, another act that Congress had already prohibited. The scandal became known as the Iran-Contra Affair.

2. Reagan vetoed a comprehensive anti-apartheid bill which would have placed economic sanctions on South Africa and cut trade with the U.S. When his Republican-controlled congress overrode his veto, Reagan answered that the law "would not solve the serious problems that plague that country".

3. Arguably Reagan's most lasting legacy to international diplomacy was helping to create the Taliban and the ascendancy of its Islamic Mujahidin leader, Osama Bin Laden. While fighting a proxy war against the Soviet Union, Reagan trained, equipped and funded the Islamist fighters in Afganistan, giving them billions of dollars, top-secret intelligence and sophisticated weapons. His willingness to continue funding this war, even after the Soviets retreated, played a direct role in Bin Laden's rise to power.

Newly released (2013) CIA intelligence documents prove that Ronald Reagan already knew that Iragi President Saddam Hussein was going to use chemical weapons against Iran during the Iran/Iraq War as early as 1983. By the time Reagan would leave office, he and his mideast allied would be responsible for thousands of deaths directly from sarin and mustard gas offensives in the region.

It comes as no surprise that on the day of Reagan's inauguration he overslept and when compelled to get up, he responded, "Do I have to?" FYI … Ronald Reagan hosted the popular "GE Theater" on TV back in the 50's. It was his embracing of the conservative views of the company which wrote his paychecks and his subsequent relationship with General Electric's Vice President Lemuel Boulware, whose core business tenets were free markets, lower taxes for business and limited government oversight, that lead to Reagan's switch to the Republican party in 1962 and his successful bid for the California governor's office in 1966. The same year (1980) that my dad and I built the hybrid energy home in Connecticut and President Jimmy Carter promoted U.S. energy independence and sustainability, our contrived hero Ronald Reagan, upon winning the Presidency, "tore down" the solar collectors from the White House and dismantled the governments incentives to make America an energy independent nation. I give up, whose hero is he?

In post - Reagan America almost every state or federal road, highway, bridge, intersection, interchange, parkway, parking lot, welcome center, building, monument, cafeteria, walking path, nature preserve, shuttle bus, and coffee mug is named after some military hero. Why is it that, in my lifetime, we've had to rely on Progressives and Democrats to dig us out of the hapless and irresponsible economic and military experiments of their Republican counterparts? In varying degrees, it has happened to Lyndon Johnson, Jimmy Carter, Bill Clinton and now Barack Obama.

Meanwhile, guess how many monuments to Peace there are in the United States? Well, there's the 352 ft. tall Perry's Victory and International Peace Memorial off the shore of Put-in-Bay, Ohio on South Bass Island where back in the 60's, pacifists and hippies (including this hippie) went to make their case for ending the Vietnam War and to play Frisbee and get high. Problem is, the Perry Memorial was commissioned back in 1912 to actually celebrate the U.S. Navy's first victory in the Battle of Lake Erie aboard the "Niagara."   So; no actual peace monument here.

Officially, there's exactly ONE…and it's technically not a peace monument either, because it celebrates naval accomplishments during the War of the Rebellion. This single "official" peace monument of the American people, located at the foot of the U.S. Capitol where Pennsylvania Avenue ends, was constructed in Rome, Italy in 1877 and placed on a marble pedestal at it's present location the same year. And there it has remained, unfinished and unappreciated for 135 years. You read that correctly. The politics of peace are so untenable and un-tellable in America that not one Congress or President since Rutherford B. Hayes has had the will or fortitude to even finish the job. It took a national tragedy for our precious monument to grab the attention of the Washington Post. In 2012, after the Newtown Connecticut massacre, the paper decided to use the site on it's cover to represent the sentiment our country felt for its loss.

State and congressional leaders, I urge you to rise to the occasion. Mr. President, make America proud. Finish the job that has eluded all of your predecessors for 135 years. I'll be happy to assist in any way I can.

The sole "official" and unfinished peace monument of the American people celebrating the War of the Rebellion.

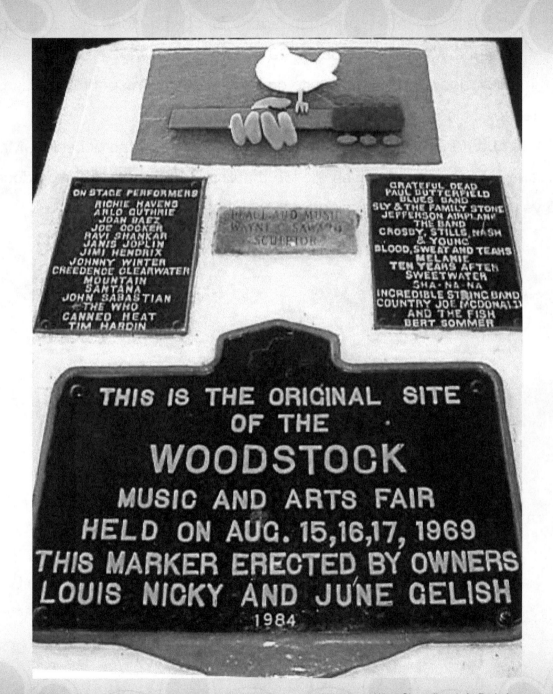

The Woodstock Music & Arts Fair monument at the corner of Hurd and West Shore Roads in Bethel, New York.

chapter seven
FROM FAMILY FARM TO WATER FEATURE

"All the weary mothers of the earth will finally rest

We will take their babies in our arms and do our best

When the sun is low upon the field

To love and music they will yield

And the weary mothers of the earth shall rest

And the farmer on his tractor and beside his plow

Will stand there in confusion as we wet his brow

With the tears of all the businessmen

Who see what they have done to him

And the weary farmers of the earth shall rest

And the aching workers of the world again shall sing

These words in mighty choruses to all will bring

'We shall no longer be the poor

for no one owns us anymore'

And the workers of the world again shall sing

And when the soldiers burn their uniforms in every land

The foxholes at the borders will be left unmanned

General, when you come for the review

The troops will have forgotten you

And the men and women of the earth shall rest"

— *Joan Baez, 1971-1972 (Chandos Music, ASCAP)*

Alan Gerry's climb to the top of the A list as one of America's wealthiest men began back in the 1950's when, as a high school dropout, he joined the Marines and learned electronics and television repair through the G.I. Bill. That knowledge and the introduction of fiber-optics technology gave Gerry the incentive, in his rural Liberty, New York, to step in and literally own what, to date, had been the free transmission of broadcast TV. And own it he did. Founding Cablevision in 1951, at the inception of the media's meteoric ascent, he helped pioneer microwave distribution of the signals in remote regions of the country. By 1996, Gerry's $20,000 investment had earned him 2.7 billion dollars when Time Warner decided it was ready to buy him out. Alan Gerry was, hands down, one of the 1% by 2007. But that's not what's "got my goat" about Mr. Gerry.

On the weekend of August 15, 16 and 17, 1969, the Gerry family was living in Liberty, New York less than a 15 minute drive from Yasgur's Farm. When Alan's teenage daughter told her father that she wanted to go to the Woodstock event, Alan was livid. These were dirty and degenerate hippies who did drugs and had no regard for decency. He blatantly forbid her to go. His daughter defied him and went anyway. No doubt that similar stories played out in many upstate New York households that weekend but the Alan and Sandra Gerry family feud would take on national significance when, in 1996, father Alan sealed the deal to purchase 2,000 acres including the 600 acre Yasgur's Farm with the intent of turning the natural rolling landscape into a Disney-esque corporation, performing arts museum and future condo. If Alan hated Woodstock so much that he refused to let his own daughter participate, what was he doing buying the place? I could only imagine it to be greed, corporate myopia or plain old vindication. As you will soon discover, my efforts to interact with Gerry's once bucolic "Woodstock" turned faux friendly, antithetical, Ultra-high security, corporate, pseudo groovy personal money maker, would reach an unimaginable impasse as the chase continued.

Every five years, since our 1984 realization of the Original Woodstock Program

Project's significance in both American and Rock and Roll history, Linda and I had returned to Yasgur's Farm to join with thousands of veterans of the iconic event, as well as many more thousand who had come to learn and share the ideology and magic that was the essence of Woodstock's unintended symbiosis. Just a couple of years prior to that realization, we were returning to Vermont from a business meeting in New Jersey when we noticed that our route took us unavoidably close to White Lake. We decided spontaneously to see if we could finally locate the famed concert site. We came into the area on a north/south state road and when it intersected the main highway, we pulled into a local auto repair shop and gas station to ask for help. A young mechanics helper approached. "We're looking for the original site of Woodstock, can you give us directions from here?" I might as well have been speaking French. I went on. "You know, the famous concert that drew a half a million people." He vaguely recalled the whole affair and solicited the help of the shop's owner. "Hey Joe, you know how to get to where that concert was back in the 60's?" Joe, it turned out, was only slightly more helpful. "Go across there, go down there, past the lake, take a left and just keep going." We thanked him anyway and, well, just kept going! Passing the lake, the road turned to dirt and somehow we ended up on the dead end, private drive of a chicken farmer. Reversing course at the sole intersection, our perseverance and intuition suddenly revealed a small lake on our left, followed by a lush rolling corn field ready for harvesting. Our car seemed to stop on it's own. We were in the middle of nowhere, on a dirt road with not a house or sign in sight. I turned to Linda and said, "This is it."

"Where?" she challenged.

"That corn field right there," I retorted, as if an expert on the topic.

We left the car along the road, doubting that another would be along anytime soon, and headed up into the seven foot high corn. Approaching the midway point on the hill, it became clear that we were in fact not alone. We saw a young couple and began, in a most casual way, to ask them if our intuition was correct. "Yes," they declared in unison. Now there were four, on the crystal clear summer day. "Down there is where the stage was," they explained. "This spot is where we met, that weekend. We return to this garden every year as a celebration of our love." We spoke of the serendipity of the moment and just took in the euphoric, sensual, stimuli that is nature's gift. A glance down at the road below revealed we had more company. Two compact cars were parked where twenty minutes ago there was one. The driver, traveling alone, had seen us from the road and was on his way up to join the "love in." He too recounted the significance of that historic weekend and told us that he returns every year on the anniversary. "When's that?" I inquired. "This is it," he replied. "No way," I interjected. If I had been a theist, it could have easily been a sign from above; perhaps a miracle. It was neither. Instead, moments later, the sign we received was from below, on the door of the next car on the scene, NBC News.

A cameraman and a reporter emerged from the now three car traffic pile-up and started in our direction. "Hi, how are you guys? Mind if we interview you for the anniversary of Woodstock?" Lin and I remained inconspicuous, not having gone and still unaware of the logistics behind the Program. When asked, we repeated the events of the day, expressed our joy just being in the moment and listened intently to the recollections of the others. The NBC guys handled themselves in a poised and professional manner and were gone as abruptly as they had arrived. It was now mid-afternoon and we still had a three hour drive back to central Vermont but, before departing, we all agreed to meet back at the 20th. "Oh, and when we do, I'll bring my copy of the Program that was given out at the concert," I suggested. "What program? There were no programs,"I was told. "See you in '89."

After stopping for dinner, we arrived back home later than anticipated but emotionally charged by the day's experience. The NBC Nightly News was just going on from the Albany affiliate. "Up next," the anchor announced, "Celebrating the anniversary of Woodstock at Yasgur's Farm." We had made the national news.

I was a little skeptical about bringing the original program with me to the 15th year reunion, so, to be safe, I made up a full color copy of the document, bound it together and headed down the New York State Thruway. There was no formal event planned for the weekend, just come as you are and enjoy the moment. I think that of all the reunions we've attended, this 15th was the most sociologically inspiring and sincere. By 1984, the land had already been sold by the Yasgur family to Loius Necketopoulis. That same year, June Gelish, Louis' lover, from Brooklyn, New York, erected the Monument, at the southeast corner of the Hurd Rd. intersection, adjacent to the original stage and staging area for the concert. When we arrived at that precise location on the weekend of August 14 & 15, 1984, the monument was brand new and the center of interest for all who pilgrimage back to the garden. The day was bright sunshine and one by one people from every conceivable walk of life made their way down Hurd Rd. I'd be surprised if the crowd ever numbered more than 1,500 but, here's the thing; the dialogue was open and abundant, the mood was exuberant and the time flew by. No one asked you what kind of car you drove or how much money you made. No one cared about your race, nationality or religious affiliation. We were there to, well, just be there and share that feeling together, a sense of purpose and belonging that only the right combination of nature and human empathy can create.

Linda and I returned often to the monument where, upon our arrival, I had placed the color copy of The Program. By early afternoon, it had been picked up so frequently that the binding was starting to fray. We were attentive to the interest it was getting and it didn't take long to realize that almost everyone was seeing it for the first time. I began to wonder myself, how did I end up with this beautiful, 50 page, color booklet that must have cost a fortune to design and print, when nobody else, including Woodstock attendees, ever saw or heard of it? The mystery would begin to dissolve with the arrival of one Mr. Wavy Gravy. Wavy was the emcee of the original concert and had returned to celebrate the occasion. A brief personal encounter with the legend helped me to begin the process of rediscovery. He told me that he had two copies himself but they were in pretty bad shape. He recalled that they had been brought back stage, toward the end of the concert. He said he thought that few had survived. It was at that moment I knew I had to do something extraordinary to share this historic document with the world and the logical place to start would be with the artists themselves. Every artist who was scheduled to appear on stage that historic weekend had a featured page or shared page in this pop art and paisley graphic masterpiece. But, how many of them even knew that their moment at Woodstock had been so professionally documented. And, by 1984, who knew where on earth they were or how to gain access to them. I had my mission.

Wavy Gravy photo: Hugh Romney, aka, Wavy Gravy talks about the Woodstock Program at the 20th Anniversary, Yasgur's Farm 1989.

THE ORIGINAL woodstock PROGRAM

PROJECT

© 1994 R & L Evans, VT

ONE CONCERT / ONE PROGRAM
ONE WEEKEND THAT CHANGED HISTORY
August 15, 16 & 17, 1969

JOAN BAEZ
THE BAND
BLOOD, SWEAT and TEARS
CANNED HEAT
JOE COCKER
COUNTRY JOE & THE FISH
CREEDENCE CLEARWATER REVIVAL
CROSBY, STILLS and NASH
GRATEFUL DEAD
ARLO GUTHRIE
TIM HARDIN
KEEF HARTLEY
RICHIE HAVENS
JIMI HENDRIX
INCREDIBLE STRING BAND
IRON BUTTERFLY
WAVEY GRAVEY

JEFFERSON AIRPLANE
JANIS JOPLIN
JOSHUA LIGHT SHOW
MELANIE
MOUNTAIN
QUILL
JOHN SEBASTIAN
SANTANA BLUES BAND
SHANANA
RAVI SHANKAR
SLY and THE FAMILY STONE
BERT SOMMER
SWEETWATER
TEN YEARS AFTER
THE WHO
JOHNNY WINTER

The Original Woodstock Program Project artist tee shirt circa 1994. Can you identify the group that performed at Woodstock, but never made it onto the artist commemorative tee shirt list?

chapter eight

REACHING FOR THE STARS

Ben Cohen, left, & Jerry Greenfield, right, childhood friends open their first ice cream shop in a renovated gas station in downtown Burlington, Vermont in 1978.

ben, jerry, arlo, & the band

By the spring of 1993, Lin and I began in earnest to piece together the mystery of the Woodstock Program. Nearly a half a million people attended the most famous Rock & Roll concert in American history, yet most everyone I queried gave the same unapprised answer, "There were no programs!"

A call to Better Music in New York City on June 29th would finally reveal the truth. I was in search of Lee Blumer. She had been Michael Lang's secretary during the summer of 1969 when he, Artie Kornfeld, John Roberts and Joel Rosenman put together Woodstock Ventures for the purpose of raising funds for the Woodstock, New York arts society. Lee told me that she was responsible for handling the production and distribution of the Program for Lang, et al. "There were 35,000 copies printed," she explained. The truck carrying these beautiful four color, 50 page Aquarian Exposition Concert Programs left the New Jersey printers on Friday morning August 15th, 1969 expecting to deliver them by 11 am. the same day, but ended up, instead, getting stuck in the same 10 mile long traffic snarl as almost everyone else. It would be late Sunday afternoon amidst a torrential downpour and a mass exodus from the site before the delivery truck would find its way to the intended back stage drop zone. Without regard for the contents, case after case was thrown down into the mud to be wrapped in a legacy for the ages.

After the phone call, it all began to make sense. At best, perhaps a few of the artists who were still around backstage Sunday may have acquired a copy of the abandoned programs. There seemed only one way to find out.

In 1990, Vermont's own Ben Cohen and Jerry Greenfield, known to the rest of America as "Ben & Jerry's Ice Cream," began sponsoring their "One World – One Heart Festival" in Warren, Vermont, home to Sugarbush Ski Area... Eternally true to their employees and themselves, Vermont's most famous hippies found a way to keep the dream and political awareness going, year after year. Among the creative methods they embraced was a booth to write a note to your congressmen or legislator postage paid. Your reward for participating in the democratic process, a FREE ice cream cone. Can't beat that!

We arrived mid-morning. Thousands were already in attendance at the ski area base lodge outdoor stage and yet somehow a sense of intimacy always prevailed. A common cause, an air of peace, a sense of belonging, a Vermont state of well-being and of progressive like-mindedness. One imagines the feeling of tranquility that the Trapp Family must have experienced in their "Sound of Music" relocation from a war-torn Austria to another time and place, just a few miles up the road from here. This year's event featured Arlo Guthrie and The Band, among other regional favorites. It was time to take the first big step.

Extra care was now given the Woodstock Program by placing it in a 9X12 manila envelope and tucking it securely under my arm. I was a man on a mission. Bond…James Bond. We worked our way into the crowd, glancing clandestinely from stage left to slope left hoping to catch a glimpse of someone acting "famous" or maybe wearing something "Official". In fact, I had no idea what I was doing. But I did know that patience was a virtue. We filled out a few congressional post cards, coped a squat on the lawn for an up close and olfactory experience of The Band's, "The Night They Drove Old Dixie Down" and "The Weight," then with program safely in tow, made our way up slope to the back of the venue. As the crowd thinned and the ski slope steepened, I glanced to my left and there on the grassy shoulder, removed from the clamor and volume below, was Mr. Arlo Guthrie and family. This was it. We approached slowly….casually, holding our proximal distance but wanting to join the conversation underway. That moment came in short order. Arlo turned, while still seated on the lawn, to acknowledge our presence. I introduced myself by name, then Linda. Taking up seats beside Arlo while removing my Program from its protective wrap, I began explaining my mission. The black-eyed susan daisey cover triggered an immediate reaction to my question, "Have you ever seen this ? " Turns out Arlo was backstage at Woodstock when the programs arrived. " I have two of these back home but one is in pretty bad shape having been passed around with friends and doused with tea, coffee and more than a few ashes," he asserted I asked if he'd be willing to sign my copy. He went straight to his dedicated page, next to that of Jimi Hendrix and with the pen I offered him wrote "Love and Peace, Arlo Guthrie."

As we made our way back down the hill toward the stage I couldn't help but think – that was easy. If all the artists are as cordial and personable as Arlo, this is going to be a real fun project. With that prediction newly ensconced in my brain, the next order of business was to find the contact person for The Band. They were just finishing up their set as we approached a Ben & Jerry's volunteer, stage left. "Talk to Joe Forno," we are told, "He's out in the crowd somewhere." We worked our way in until face to face with Joe. After summarizing the details of our mission with The Band's road manager, we certainly didn't see this one coming. "How do I know that you are not going to use this commercially or for profit?" Joe shot back. "Well, um, uh, we're just doing it for ourselves and sharing it with the bands," I explained. "You'll have to do better than that I'm afraid. Sorry no dice. Get me a guarantee of non-commercial use and we'll talk." Joe concludes. Access Denied! Talk about emotional whiplash. Shit. Maybe this wasn't going to be so easy after all.

When we returned to our mill home, I placed a call to our dear friend and legal adviser A.J. Taylor. Jeff had the solution to our first obstacle. "You want a Grantors Certificate," he explained. Keep it simple with fill-in-the-blanks. I would get to see if this easiest of answers would score a home run only two weeks later. On July 4th, The Band was scheduled to perform at Stratton Mountain Ski Resort just an hour south. With both the Original Woodstock Program and the newly minted Grantors Certificate now upgraded to a baby soft fawn leather over shoulder attaché which Linda had given me for my birthday, we approached the ticket window with a contact name and a renewed sense of optimism. We were led into the concert by way of base lodge hallways and at its conclusion given access to the garden terrace where the press and guests of the band had gathered. I focused in on Joe, docs in hand. "Remember me? I approached you a couple of weeks ago up at Ben & Jerry's concert. You said that you needed proof of non-commercial use. This is for you."

I handed over the signed and dated form. Acknowledging our having met before, Joe glanced down at the document, looked me straight in the eye with a smile of approval on his face and uttered those magic words, "Follow me!" Past security, through the backstage gate and in an instant I was surrounded by Garth Hudson, Rick Danko and Levon Helm. As they each signed The Band's yellow and black paisley page, they explained to us that they too had stayed late at Woodstock and each had very badly worn copies acquired back stage Sunday night, August 17th, 1969. Levon was the most gregarious and talkative of the three and we ended up paging through the Program with him. The conversation was more about the graphics and design of the Program and where we wanted to go with it. We thanked them for signing and for their contribution to our culture. It was a warm, sunny and calm summer afternoon on a Vermont mountaintop as we shared stories, had some laughs, mostly about the condition of The Bands copies of the Woodstock programs they had acquired backstage at Yasgur's Farm. I must admit that this was the first time I felt the urge to give back to those artists for having given so much to us; a generation in search of itself. Thanks Garth, Rick and Levon. You guys inspired the T-shirts.

Arlo's program page with signed Ben & Jerry's "One World" Tee.

johnny winter

If you have never seen the video of Johnny Winter performing "Meantown Blues" at Woodstock on Sunday evening, August 17th, 1969, you must now. If ever there was a case for genetic symbiosis and perfection, this is it. I am convinced that he must have been born with a guitar in hand. Watch his fingering. I would need three hands to press the frets he reaches with ease. His voice becomes one with the strings. No grimace, no work…he morphs into his instrument and exudes the blues.

Johnny was booked into the Stratton Mountain concert series just weeks after our successful meeting with Levon and Company. This one was going to be easy. Lin and I had partied with Johnny and his brother Edgar years before on our home turf in Connecticut. With our venue contacts and renewed incentive to succeed, we return to Stratton, arriving early on yet another gorgeous summer day. Management was once again gracious and cooperative. With little delay, we were escorted to the back of the stage where we found ourselves virtually alone. The ski area's main base lodge was behind us. The back of the concert stage maybe 40 feet in front of us and the audience partially canopied but mostly outside as the lawn seating spread upslope. Low and behold we were not alone; right behind Johnny and out of view of everyone except Lin and me was another couple busy groping each other and generally getting it on. I thought it best to leave them to their fun and wait patiently for Johnny to finish the set. With only two couples waiting to see him, this was sure to be a piece of cake. I mean, how cool was this? Two very privileged couples enjoying this amazing Johnny Winter concert from right behind the artist when suddenly the other couple left. Even better. We would greet Johnny ourselves as he descended the stage. One last encore now and we were ready... With program opened to Johnny's page and pen in hand, he took his final bows, put down his Gibson Firebird and headed straight for us. Suddenly, from out of nowhere, charging up to the stage steps from behind in virtual silence, an electric golf cart with guess who driving? It's the groper! He pulled up to the bottom the steps. Johnny hopped into the passenger seat. I go into action. "Hi Johnny, I'm Ron Evans and this is my wife Linda. We are doing the Woodstock Program Project and we would be honored if you would sign your page for us," I announced as I handed him the pen. Johnny smiled approvingly, took the pen and just as he began to write, the golf cart driver snatched the pen out of his hand, turned to me defiantly and announced "Not today!" then hit the throttle and sped off. I barely snagged the Program back from Johnny as they booked out the door. WTF.

joan baez
PART ONE

There's a saying in our rural central Vermont region, "What happens here, stays here, but not much happens here." Then there is the T-shirt I once traded with a local that read, "Clarendon, Vermont – 3 and one half miles from nowhere!" It featured a crude sketch of a country store and a scruffy red-neck getting into a beat up old pickup truck loaded with fishing and hunting paraphernalia. It would have been easy to conclude that I was hopelessly removed from my destiny. But…your destiny is what you make it.

This year, just weeks before we had arranged to catch up

with the legendary Joan Baez, a young New Yorker named Ron Ferro, following his dream, opened a breakfast café right smack dab in the middle of "Nowhere." He called it "Over Easys" and it was an instant small town success. Located midway between Ludlow and Rutland made it the closest eatery to our home and Ron's personal touch to his breakfast and lunch menu soon beckoned us back again and again (Over Easys would later gain national recognition as the place where on May 24th, 2001, shortly after W's gifting of the Presidential election, Senator Jim Jeffords chose to announce his historic defection from the Republican party. The move would alter the balance of power in the U.S. Congress and really piss off the already unpopular and blundering Bush).

On this particular beckoning, in June, a vehicle parked in front of Spring Lake Ranch caught my eye and I veered off the road to check it out. This was a real rust bucket that seemed to be pieced together using a variety of car model parts and earth tone colors. In its entirety, the predominant color was overwhelmingly "rust." I guessed it to be maybe a 1967 Dodge Valliant but I'd never seen a vehicle so devoid of actual paint, yet structurally sound. Emblazoned along the entire side of the car from front to back in bold, hand painted, san serif letters were the words "Diamonds & Rust.". I left a note for the absent driver explaining that I was scheduled to meet up with Joan Baez in a just a couple of weeks and would love to share a picture of the car with her. Joan's production company, I had recently discovered, was called Diamonds & Rust Productions. This car had to be owned by a Baez lover.

The response to my note was already on my home answering machine upon my return. "Hi, this is Becki. You left a note on my car today." My suspicions were true. Becki was a passionate Joan Baez fan and preceeded to explain how she had found this old Dodge Dart and decided to teach herself how to do car repair with it as her victim. First she rebuilt the motor, then the transmission and finally a little body work using spare parts from a variety of Dodge models. The result was a reliable ride around town and a spirited, form follows function, amalgamation of steel and primer that was the perfect tribute to our Woodstock idol. I asked Becki if she would like to send a note to Joan. Here is what she typed:

"When I drive down the road, people honk and wave. Sometimes they yell things out the window, but I can never pick out what it is. I figure some are Joan Baez fans, some are Patty Larkin fans, some are Dodge Dart fans and some are just amazed that it still runs. Sometimes people say, "I can see the rust, but where are the diamonds?" The diamonds are under the hood. I rebuilt the engine in "85, mostly just to learn how and I rebuilt the transmission in "89, because it was loud and obnoxious. Diamonds and Rust has taught me almost everything I know about cars and taken me everywhere I've wanted to go. Thank you Joan for your music and for your songs. They have enriched my life. My favorite song is "Miracles" though none can sing it except you and it took me years to find out what a "Manzanita" is. We all hope to see you in Vermont again soon."

Sincerely, Rebecca Bates

Meanwhile, still exempt from and refusing to live with a personal home computer, my people networking and land line telephone researching was getting more and more difficult. By the early 90's, everything was making the leap to cyberspace. Painfully slow and increasingly arduous, the research for a more direct link to Joan led me to the William Morris Agency and an empathetic ear who informed me of The Association of Talent Agents and The National Association of Performing Arts Managers and Agents. They in turn led me to Pollstar, the "Holy Grail" of insider information for the entertainment industry. For a good chunk of change, the addresses, phone numbers and contact info for virtually every artist and entertainer in the world could be mine. The hitch; I had to be an industry insider or professional to qualify. It was time to print up a few letterheads!

The Agency Roster for 1993 set me back over 100 big ones. That was a lot of money for a couple struggling to save a Vermont State Historic District without a trust fund. But it got me to William Morris, which got me to Diamonds & Rust, which got me to Nancy Lutzow, Joan Baez' personal secretary, which got me to Stratton Mountain on July 31st and the first of several private audiences with one of the great poetic voices of the Woodstock generation.

The anticipation of going back stage after Joan's performance has erased any memory of the actual performance or play list for July 31st, 1993. But ask about the moment we met and every detail has been safely stored in its own permanently creased cranial lock-box.

After the show, Joan's road manager, Crook Stewart, gathered up about a dozen media and private guests and walked us into a private section of the Stratton base lodge. He explained that Joan would be in shortly and that she would greet us individually. When next we saw him he was following Joan into the room, standing by her for any needed assistance. The consummate professional and watchful eye, Crook was prepared with a number of different size, shape and color writing instruments for her to choose from. This was a class act. They seemed to enjoy the moment as much as we did. I watched them work in perfect syncopation. Joan approached each person or group in the room, actually introducing herself. Lin and I hung back hoping to be the last two. Maybe that way, I gathered, she wouldn't feel rushed to move on. Joan concluded the meet and greet by approaching Lin and me with hand extended. "Hi, I'm Joan" she offered. We returned the formality and thanked her for seeing us. So many thoughts and questions run through your mind at moments like this but in the end you find yourself staying on message and cutting to the chase. We summarized the Woodstock Program Project and while passing the document to Joan, asked her if she had been aware of its existence. She shook her head. "No." It didn't take her long to find her own full, star-studded, super graphic typestyle page with accompanying verse. "Would it embarrass you if I told you I love you" gadfly… big heart hopes from

Joanie in the land of milk and truncheons; sorrowful sixties braced by folky true steel beams….OVERCOME!* (Joan Baez "Farewell Angelina")

Joan looked at Crook. He spread an array of pens and markers out in his fingers as a card player would a deck of cards. Joan chose a medium black marker and after carefully signing the bottom right corner, continued paging through the psychedelic and paisley images cover to cover as we told her how we came about acquiring it. Crook smiled and nodded in approval and although I wanted to hug her, I extended both hands to envelope her one hand instead. Perhaps another time. At that moment, I was the luckiest guy on the planet.

Several weeks later, Linda and I were invited for dinner by our friends Dick & Bridgette down Rte 7 in Danby. As we began recounting the Joan Baez story over wine and hors d'oeuvres, Bridgette stopped us cold. "Oh my god, I was watching a talk show on TV last week and Joan was one of the guests. She talked about having recently seen the original program from Woodstock and about how beautifully detailed it is." Thanks Joan. You are the definition of class.

P.S. We mailed the Diamonds & Rust picture to Joan a few days later. In subsequent conversations with Nancy, she told me that Joan had loved the picture so much that she had it hanging on the wall in her office. I was so happy for Becki. Note: In a (2013) follow up conversation with Becki's partner I was told that the rust had eventually won out and that Diamonds & Rust was no more. So it goes.

the tee

Over the long Vermont winter, Lin and I thought often about what we should be doing to make the Program Project more inviting, more appealing, more interactive for the artists. What were we missing? One by one the answers came together. First, we needed to start photo journaling our meetups. I was able to purchase a small Olympus camera from a relative in Tucson, Arizona for $25.00. It was as compact as a digital but used 35mm film. Very cool little camera, easy to carry, awesome German lens. But, you know what this meant? We now had to go back and see if we could arrange a re-visit with Joan, Arlo and The Band. Setting that thought aside for the time being, what else were we missing? What was standard fare at all the recording sessions, concert venues, and band member hang-outs? Then it hit us; black T-shirts, with white lettering, of course. The un-official uniform of the official rock and roll aficionado! If we could come up with a simple yet creative image that represented the essence of both the Woodstock experience and the Program and if we could give one to each of the artists who participated by signing and granting us an interview, it would be something special to share and, at once, a means of saying thanks for the music. I asked Linda if she would be willing to come up with something. I wanted the best. Well, OK, I may be slightly biased but I think she nailed it. Our first run of only a dozen shirts, mostly large and x-large with a couple of mediums thrown in for us would not make it off the silk screen press before the next Woodstock legend came a rolling into town.

The official Program Tee with famous Landy poster in the Woodstock & vinyl room.

richie havens

An advertisement in the Rutland Herald, the nation's oldest family-owned daily newspaper, told of a visit by Mr. Richie Havens to the central Vermont inter-mountain hamlet of Randolph, with one stoplight, a music box museum and a population of 4,800. This could be reminiscent of the old Harry Chapin days of high school gyms and coffee houses. I called for tickets and to see if I could arrange a few moments with the artist. "I don't think you will have any problem, but I'll pass the word on to his agent," I was told.

When we arrived it was even better than I could have hoped for. Seating was first come with folding wooden chairs and an audience capacity of maybe 300. The announcement was made that Richie would be coming out at the conclusion of the performance to meet us and sign autographs.

This presentation was like being invited to Richie Havens' house and a private concert for a few hundred of his closest friends. He talked about hanging out in Greenwich Village in the 60s, going from coffee house to coffee house to showcase his music…getting around by bicycle. Ritchie's soulful acoustic rhythms are a product of his strong capo-ed cords, his jeweled wall of treble sound steadily eating away at the face of his guitar and his deep, raspy, haunting voice. He shared stories of Woodstock. The ride in by helicopter, the images etched in his mind's eye, having been the first artist on stage and the improvisation of "Freedom" that would remain his enduring moment.

Once again we waited to be last to meet our Woodstock legend. Richie was warm and engaging. Dressed in his signature African Dashikis and possessing a million dollar smile to match his gold and diamond necklaces and rings, he proudly added his signature to the Program. With Olympus in hand he would become our first photo documentation.

• Ten years later, on September 25th, 2004 our friend and Rutland, Vermont native, Rick Redington, was invited to open for Richie Havens at the Lebanon Opera House in Lebanon, New Hampshire . We dropped in early and found an open door in the back of the building. As we climbed the stairs leading backstage, I kept calling "Is anyone here, HELLO?" Approaching the top, one voice bellowed the answer. "Hey, welcome. I remember you guys. Come on in and have some fruit." I introduced my cousins Jesse and Peter, who were visiting from Phoenix, to our host for the evening, the gracious and incomparable Mr. Richie Havens. We spent the next uninterrupted half hour, before Rick Reddington's arrived, talking one on one with the Woodstock legend, sharing his stories of the historic event and our ongoing chase.

• Richie was adorned with the least amount of jewelry I had ever seen him wear, which was still substantial by societal norms. Backstage he had not added the extra bling needed to create that very distinct tympanic rhythm so unique to his performances.

• Our convivial host suggested that we dive into the fruit bowl prepared for him and set centered on an institutional style wood top table in the middle of the room. "Grab a drink and have a seat," Richie insisted. "Rick should be here shortly," he added. "So, how's the Woodstock project going?" As much as I wanted to share details of all the Woodstock legends our chase had brought us together with, I was greatly distracted by the fact that I was in the presence of the one and only "Freedom" hero of Yasgur's Farm; the first performer to face the overwhelming crowd on August 15th, 1969. On this day we were a crowd of four, alone with our idol.

• It didn't take long for us to re-direct Richie back to talking about Richie. "I know you're from New York, Richie," I offered, "but tell us about your early days there." He recalled moving from Brooklyn, his birth place, into the city as a teenager. "The draw was the culture of art and artist. I began going from club to club in the Village looking to perform while still working at a florist shop during the day." Richie's transportation mode of choice was his ten speed bike. I remember being in Greenwich Village back in 1968 with a small group of friends when suddenly Richie Havens came flying past us on that very bike. He was gone in a flash. I relayed that story to him as we sat around the fruit bowl backstage. Richie let out one of his deep bass exuberant laughs. It was pure Richie. "That was me," he announced proudly.

Thanks, Richie. I'll never forget your warm smile and kind demeanor.

paint
*the frescoed images by way
of harsh black grandeur
and sliding harkening will'o worlds
to further parts of haven*

RICHIE HAVENS

Richard Pierce Havens (January 21,1941 - April 22, 2013).

crosby stills & nash

We began to feel like industry insiders as preparations got underway to meet up with our heroes of Laurel Canyon, David Crosby, Steven Stills and Graham Nash. If this had been scheduled for any other venue I would have tried the pragmatic agency approach, but SPAC was different. As our Program Project evolved, it became increasingly clear that, for everything to go smoothly, timing, venue site and the inevitable unexpected intervening variable had to be anticipated. In other words, "Good luck with that!"

By now we were on a first name basis with most of the

key players in Saratoga. Coleen in security, John in production and Will at the gate were all rooting for us when we arrived early in the afternoon while the grounds were still open. Will brought us backstage to John. John introduced us to Richard Fernandez, CS&N's road manager. Richard issued us our first ever "After Show" passes and comp seats for the concert. We headed into town for an early dinner as the anticipation heightened. Seriously? We could hardly eat. We were about to be the guests of the most harmonic, poetic, male messengers of our generation and it all began with a parental act of kindness.

The Saratoga Performing Arts Center's 10 story, 5,100 seat amphitheater is located within the 2,400 pristine acres of the Saratoga Spa State Park and is host to the New York City Ballet and The Philadelphia Philharmonic Orchestra. But starting on September 1st in 1968 a rock performance by Jim Morrison and The Doors would begin a tradition that continues to this day.

Our tickets and passes were waiting for us at "Will Call" as Richard promised. By show time the house was near capacity and the outdoor lawn seats numbered at least twice that many. Saratoga would be only the third and final venue this year to host CS&N with Fleetwood Mac as the opening act. I must admit that my efforts were so focused once again on meeting up with our hosts that an otherwise memorable Fleetwood performance went virtually un-noticed. It came back in snippets as research for literary accuracy herein labored on.

CS&N ran through one hit after another, interspersing work from their new album "After the Storm," scheduled for release the following week. David Crosby continued his policy of interjecting on-stage political commentary while Graham and Steven did most of the audience P.R. work. It became clear, as the concert progressed, that David was having a tough go of it and was struggling to make it through. At the show's conclusion, he was the first one off. As the audience meandered toward the rear exits, Linda and I moved forward to the stage left post we had been instructed to go to. A group of perhaps two dozen "After Show" pass holders were held here by security for what seemed like forever. It was in real time 15 minutes. We used the wait to run through our project protocol. Program, check. Pens, check. Camera, check. Camera with film in it, check. T-Shirt, check. (I was proudly wearing my size medium for the first time).

The word came from backstage. This was it. We were led down the hallway past the infamous "Santana Intersection," only this time instead of taking a left toward the dressing rooms, we were directed to turn right and into a conference/cafeteria room. What we saw was a scene straight out of "Access Hollywood" or " The Oscars" minus the red carpet. There must have been 100 band member friends, media personalities, reporters and you name it, jammed into I'm guessing a 40'X50' space. The decibel level seemed to exceeded that of the concert. Stay focused. What to do? We had to talk directly into each other's ears to hear. "You see C, S or N?" I asked. We panned around the room. It was clear that we were not the first ones in this night. A feeling of urgency arose. Suddenly I caught a glimpse of Graham. He was smack in the middle of the room and, by all appearances, having quite the after show celebration. But wait. What was this? As we worked our way in, the scene began to look more like an Arts Fair. Table-top displays and kiosks were scattered about the room with everything from Green Peace pamphlets to Bumper Stickers to Craft items. This was a show within a show and as much as we wanted to stop at every one, we had to stay focused on Graham. I waited my turn as Linda readied the camera. Here we go. Introductions made, it becomes instantly apparent why Graham was the glue that held CS&N together through so many trials and tribulations. He was cordial, warm and engaging: the kind of person who makes you feel welcomed in his company….a regular British gentleman. His eyes widen as I remove the Woodstock Program from its protective leather case and explain our mission. Linda snaps a picture. She's getting more comfortable with the Olympus as Graham pages through the Program and finds his page. My instincts tell me this is his first time but I have to ask. "No, never," he replies. He signs the thickly bordered CS&N page, poses for one more photo then reaches into his pocket and retrieves a business card that reads; Bill Brender, M.D. Turning the card over Graham writes the address and phone number of his agent and asks if I ever come across another program to please contact him directly; he would like one for himself. I accept the challenge and ask if he has seen David or Steven. We are told that David has left the venue for his hotel room, that he is not feeling too well but maybe we can catch up with Steven before he goes. Helping with our things, Graham leads us down the stage corridor. Just outside his dressing room, and on his way out the door for his hotel, we snag Steven. "Steven, check this out." And the rest, as they say, is history!

"Helplessly hoping, her harlequin hovers nearby

Awaiting a word

Grasping at glimpses of gentle free spirit he runs,

Wishing he could fly.

Only to trip at the sound of good-bye"

-Stephen Stills, 1969 (Goldhill Music)

On November 5th 1994, just two months after our Graham Nash and Steven Stills moment at SPAC, David Crosby was admitted into the hospital with liver failure. He received his controversial transplant two weeks later.

Graham Nash hand written contact info. Back stage passes and comp tics.

yargur's farm 1994

Twenty-five years later, the magic of "The Garden" and of the Yasgur's Farm legacy was still having a profound effect on those who believed in John Lennon's "Imagine" and the power of peace and music. As the corporate and political direction of the country reversed course and greater numbers of my generation sold out to the narcissism, conspicuous material consumerism and greed that would become the nouveau-American anthem, fewer sanctuaries remained.

Leading up to this weekend, the news from Bethel was that the event scheduled for Yasgur's Farm was On, then Off, then On again. As town officials there argued over permits and crowd control, Michael Lang, the brainchild of the '69 event, was busy up the road in Saugerties creating a media extravaganza with few of the original artists but with lots of corporate sponsors..

Bethel officials had finally decided that they would allow visitors and musicians back on the original site for the 25th Anniversary. We packed up our '71 VW Woodie Bug and headed down the Northway giving ourselves enough time to drop in on Lang & Co. before proceeding to Bethel. Michael's Saugerties site, which was one considered for the original Woodstock, was immediately off the New York State Thruway. Going directly to the field office, we met up with George Terpening, Head of Community Relations for Woodstock '94, who offered us a private golf cart tour of the entire concert facility just hours before it was to be opened to the public. Lining the perimeter of the Winston Farm mega-field were literally 2,800 port-a-johns, 2,000 tons of soft drink and beer, hundreds of police on horse back and more than 500 medical personnel.   North and south main stages measuring an estimated 150' across and a towering 6 stories high stood as monuments at the west side of the main field. Readied security personnel milled patiently about as we spead by on a course for the main gate. This was a well-oiled machine, we were told. Instead, what I saw was a police presence to rival a Presidential visit.. We thanked our tour guide, hopped back into our VW Woodie and made our way south to Bethel sensing that, with so much alcohol waiting to be consumed by a third of a million people, we were getting out just in the nick of time.

It was Thursday afternoon August 11th when we arrived at Yasgur's Farm. Hundreds of campers had already set up weekend accommodations along the upper ridgeline of the Garden's natural amphitheater. It was a picture- perfect day in the Catskills. We cruised the field in our VW and found a comfortable opening to suit our Coleman easy up two-person tent. Directly in front of our tent fly at a distance of maybe 25 feet was a tighter grouping of tents built around a center stonelined fire pit. A coffee pot balanced precariously on wood embers and a muted but jovial laughter coming from the gathering suggested that we are welcome here.

After setting up our own site we meandered down slope to the neighbors to get acquainted over coffee. Our conversation kept returning to one particular individual. He was easy to talk with and a storyteller extraordinaire. While brushing back his graying pony-tail, our hands met over the simmering, wood-seared coffee pot. "Hi, I'm Kevin from Yuma." We zeroed in on each other and talked for hours on everything from politics to teaching. Having taught public school math for 25 years on the Arizona/Mexico border, where he was literally the only Anglo (including faculty and student body) in his entire school, had endowed him with mediation skills equal to those of our inner-city beginnings. As more celebrants arrived, we got to put some of those skills to the test. Minor conflicts were mediated without altercations and by late in the day I had given our new friend the title of "Mayor of Woodstock." Exhausted, Linda and I crashed early ahead of all-night discussions around a fire kept glowing and warm by our newly elected Mayor.

Friday morning enveloped Yasgur's Farm in sunshine. The crowing of roosters from nearby family farms and the gradual clamor of breakfast utensils and car radios welcomed us back to the Garden. Thousands more would arrive this day. It didn't take long for the word to spread that Arlo, Melanie, Richie Havens and friends were coming tomorrow to give a free concert. Meanwhile, as the Mayor kept the home fire burning on low, thousands more arrived. They had come to be part of history; part of a yearning, part of a peaceloving community built around a moral imperative that was now etched in stone on this historic spot. By late morning, Hurd Road was a steady stream of traffic. Micro-buses, SUVs, campers, Beamers, motorcycles, an occasional Ferrari or Rolls Royce…you name it. There were no status symbols here today.

Impromptu vendors popped up everywhere. The sun held out as we made our way down the famous amphitheater slope, past the Monument and across Hurd, where we met up with Max and Mariam Yasgur's grandchildren. Jill Yasgur had flown in from Paris with a film crew documenting the 25th Anniversary for French TV, while her stateside brother Stuart was vending his commemorative Yasgur's Farm T-shirts. We hit it off right away and the hour together vanished as we talked about France, Woodstock, The Program Project, this amazing moment and coming to stay with Jill next time we visit Paris.

By the time we made it back to the campsite it was late afternoon. The heat and humidity of the midday sun was threatening showers but the Mayor's communal fire was still aglow. Until now, we had concentrated on being good listeners and had not mentioned our historic document to anyone here. That was about to change. For the first time since our arrival, we three were alone, among tens of thousands. Drawing our beach chairs in close, Lin and I began our tale. It didn't take long to realize that Kevin possessed a wealth of Woodstock knowledge. He had gone in '69 and had experienced all 4 days of the 3-day event. But for him too, the Program was an anomaly that seemed to have slipped below the radar. The Mayor's keen networking skills became immediately apparent as he laid the following on us over our afternoon siesta. "Did you guys know that Jefferson Starship was playing at The Pines in Monticello tonight?" Guess you know where we went right after dinner.

The incontrovertible swoon of the Jefferson Airplane's Marty Balin and Paul Kantner could be heard as we climbed the curved conifer-lined driveway approach leading to The Pines parking lot. The band was well into their second set when we were escorted into the theater by management. By '94 Grace Slick had gone off mostly on her own. The Slick impersonator this evening was well rehearsed as Balin and Kantner ran through one Airplane hit after another. As the Project went along, we began to get a better sense of timing and after-show protocol: 10 to 20 minutes seemed to be the window of opportunity. Any less time and the artists had not yet caught their breath. Any more time and they may very well have left the building. Within that window, management led us out of the theater and down a short outdoor pathway to a set of private cabins. The front door of the second cabin was wide open, the after show party spilling out into the sidewalk. Logistically this was no time to be last. I removed the Program from its attaché as Linda readied the camera. The two original members of Jefferson Airplane who had played on stage in 1969 were standing almost side by side in the middle of the room as I approached. It was clear that I was not going to get an interview but I did get to pose the question. Both answered "No." Two more legends of Woodstock were now officially introduced to the elusive program and both went home with t-shirts. We returned to Yasgur's Farm with our first Airplane signatures and a heightened anticipation for tomorrow's free concert.

Word had begun getting back that the Saugerties concert was having issues. The alcohol and price gouging had made for a volatile mix. This time there would be no "Officer Friendly" to smooth things out.

With the weather still holding in Bethel, Producer/Artist Richie Havens arranged to have a flatbed truck brought in and placed in the same location as the original stage. A few sheets of plywood braced and screwed in place created a makeshift platform for tonight's show. Local lead-off acts provided the equipment and by mid afternoon we were underway. Arlo arrived early. We caught up in the backstage parking area and made it quick. An impromptu photo and a T-shirt exchange and we were off. My focus was instead on an artist that was scheduled to go on later, after dark. Back in the 60s, I had a thing for cute female recording artists that seemed to expound on a progressive message for peace in their lyrics. Linda Ronstadt, Joan Baez and Melanie were among my favorites. A gentle rain began to fall as dusk turned to darkness. It couldn't have been planned more perfectly for Melanie's encore performance of "Candles in the Rain" which she had written about her original Woodstock appearance.

Immediately following her standing ovation performance, Linda and I went around the back of the flatbed stage and met up with Melanie there. She was sincere, friendly and enamored by the sight of the Program. Another Woodstock veteran seeing the official playbill of their historic life-changing appearance for the very first time. After accepting our T-shirt as our thank you, she came back to us a short time later and asked us if we would send her 3 more for her kids Beau, Leilah and Jordie. I turned over the envelope of the Program. Melanie wrote down her Safety Harbor, Florida address, where she lived then.

One last promise had to be honored before heading home. Along the Hurd Rd. ridge among the vendor vehicles was a small panel box truck with the following banner prominently displayed on its exterior, "Woodstock Program Re-prints - $10." There they were, hundreds of slightly off color reproductions of my original with an added first page stating that these were re-prints. Someone I knew had told me he really wanted one. I broke down and made the cash investment for two copies.

Sunday dawned rain free and as the sun burned the morning dew from Max's field, we packed up camp, said our goodbyes and headed home. Well, we kind of headed home. After eating camp food for three days, the White Lake Diner, five minutes away, was simply too difficult to pass up. Settling in on the last two window seats in the packed breakfast spot, we found ourselves back to back with a young writer who took notice of my T-shirt. "Hi, I'm Marty Hirsch and I'm doing a story on the Woodstock legacy. I noticed your T-shirt. Can we talk?"

Martin was trying to make rhyme or reason of the corporate direction that his life had taken since his hippie days and his attendance at the original concert. Could not one be true to ones principles while working for a major international pharma-ceutical corporation? From a vantage point of Human Resources, Martin came away from the 25th anniversary and our hour together with a tad less personal conflict. We came away with another 25-year mandate for chasing the Woodstock legacy.

Two weeks later, I was up the driveway mowing the lawn by the covered bridge at the Mill when suddenly Linda appears, phone in one hand while gesturing across her neck to shut the mower off with her other. Cupping the receiver and with a proud smile and wide eyes she whispers, "It's Graham Nash!" Holy Shit, was the first thing that popped into my mind. "Ron, Graham Nash here. I got the Program you sent me. It's great. Thank you so much for thinking of me." I reminded him that it was a reprint but it was the best I could do. "It's perfect. You take good care of the Original and my best to you and Linda." WOW. In all the years of the project, Graham alone took the time to call. I guess I shouldn't have been so surprised. I felt it the first time we met.

Kevin "The Mayor of Woodstock" Bowman retired from teaching in 2008 and has since taken on a leading role at the world famous annual "Burning Man" celebration in Nevada's high desert. If you want to meet him there, just ask for "The Mayor". There's only one.

Marty Balin (right) and Paul Kantner of Jefferson Airplane at the Pines Resort dressing room signing 1994.

Melanie, backstage at the 25th.

WOODSTOCK 94

George Terpening
Community Relations

4 Churchland Road
Saugerties, NY 12477
Telephone: 914-247-0700
Fax: 914-247-0765

HUG PASS

This card entitles the holder to
ONE FREE HUG
Payable Upon Request

Good Any Time

The Pines
RESORT HOTEL
SOUTH FALLSBURG, N.Y. 12779

Local - (914) 434-6000
FAX - (914) 434-7677

Toll Free - 1-800-367-4637

Top to bottom: Media satellite trucks at the Saugerties event. The main stage just hours before being opened to the public, 1994.

The VW Woodie and Free Hug pass at Richie Haven's sponsored Yasgur's Farm alternative free event, 1994.

Kevin "The Mayor" Bowman, Linda and me at the 25th.

Makeshift stage erected by Richie Havens for the 25th Anniversary event at Yasgur's Farm.

grateful dead

The road to Highgate lead straight through Yuma, Arizona once again. Neither Linda nor I had ever attended a Grateful Dead concert but the facts were quite the opposite for our friend Kevin. He was not just a Dead Head, he founded the Arizona Chapter of the Grateful Dead Fan Club. Kevin's loyalty to the music, free expression and counter-cultural mores of the Dead experiment were the cornerstone of who he was. Hell, he even had a section of Interstate 8 east of Yuma at the Ligurta foothills named after the band's leader Jerry Garcia. Kevin's home there was a mini shrine to the Dead. As a public school teacher with summers free, he traveled the country in pursuit of the next tour venue.

This summer, the Dead were scheduled to play a second year in the remote Vermont town of Highgate, just south of the Canadian border. The concert was expected to draw over 100,000 people to the farming community, population of 3,400, that was home to the largest egg farm in Vermont. We got the Mayor's call in May. He's flying in for the show and wants us to join him. How do we say no? He has been such a good friend and a huge help with our Project. We don't.

Could there be a more ideal set of dynamics in play for this event? With weeks to go before the concert I've got Kevin (the Mayor), the deadest deadhead of them all, flying in from Yuma; Patrick Leahy, the senior Senator from Vermont and a self-proclaimed Dead Head with an On Stage Pass for the show, to contact; and Pollstar tells me that Dennis McNally is the Dead publicist to talk to for arrangements. This one's going to be the bomb. My friend, my senator, my wife, my Program's centerfold and the entire Grateful Dead lineup. We are going to have the time of our lives.

A call to Dennis McNally revealed that the band did not have a good experience at Woodstock and rather wanted to forget the whole thing. I told him that the Program Project was not about re-living or even re-visiting the concert but instead was a personal quest that celebrates a simple act of kindness and the historic document associated with it. Dennis was unmoved. With the Highgate event now only 3 days away we decided that we would take a day trip to the Canadian border and see if we could find a welcoming ear. The concert was being staged at the site of the Franklin airport, a small aircraft launch just outside of town. As we approached checkpoint "Charlie," the security gate established by the Dead, we were asked for credentials. I went through the details of our Project but was told that there was no one on site to speak to. The six hour round trip turned out to be a complete waste of time and we would have to repeat the whole process again when The Mayor arrived from Yuma. I spent the next 48 hours trying to contact Senator Leahy, whom I had always supported and voted for, to see if I could get a sympathetic ear and perhaps a liaison with the band.

Neither he nor any member of his staff ever returned my phone calls.

Linda and I were determined to make concert day a fun time for Kevin in spite of the personal disappointments we had experienced in the lead up. The Mayor had rolled some of his famous sage incense sticks for barter with the many vendors about the grounds and even if we were not Dead aficionados ourselves, Bob Dylan was the opening act. The stage site, an open and grassed field, had been page fenced for the early evening event.

I tend to be one of those people who evaluate the logistics and dynamics that are around me at any given moment. I like being observant without being obsessive about it. The Highgate venue had been designed in a large equilateral triangular fashion with the entrance and exit gates at the narrowest end and the stage set off to one side at the distal and widest part. This gave ticket holders a wide berth once inside the concert but made for a narrow Venturi-like funnel at the conclusion. Even from the very back of the crowd we could see our esteemed senator and his friends on stage left with the band during the whole affair. I bit my tongue and rationalized the whole thing by thinking, Dylan should have quit a long time ago and Garcia and Co. can hardly carry a tune. We were with our friend and the day was beautiful, what more did we need?

Parking for Highgate was off site by as much as a mile. All ticket holders were shuttled to the venue via yellow school buses leased from the county. At the conclusion of the show 100,000 people began slowly moving toward the exits. Remember what I said about the geometry in play here. The exit gates were maybe 50 feet wide while the staging area was well over 500 feet deep. All that humanity squeezing into a tiny exit was formula enough for disaster but as we drew closer among the first wave to exit, I couldn't believe my eyes. Parked directly in front of the exit gates at a distance of less than 4 feet and literally bumper to bumper was the entire fleet of full sized school buses. A glance behind showed 85,000 people accelerating toward an exit that didn't exist. I made a plea to those behind us to pass the word back, "The exits are blocked by the buses and please stop moving forward for a little while." It seemed to be working. The squeeze diminished from behind as the crowd in front began climbing over the bus bumpers and hoods. Disaster averted, at least until the next and final time I would try to share my Project with the pseudo-atman of the Dead Franchise.

leavin' the light on

In the spring of 1995 I received an inquiry from Don and Diane Bodette in response to an ad we had taken out in the local paper for "House for rent." The historic Kingsley/Crary house, one of the oldest certifiable homes in the state, had recently been vacated. Don, the official keeper of genealogy for the Bodette name, his wife Diane and daughter Dawn took an instant liking to the 10 room, center stairway, post and beam antique even though it was, by '95, in desperate need of a total renovation. Moreover, the four of us took an instant liking to each other. Diane was a nurse's assistant at the local hospital and even though the two also owned a fulltime commercial cleaning service, Don was in search of a "project in his spare time" that would showcase his many handyman skills and keep his mind occupied. They wanted the lease and got it.

It didn't take the Bodettes long to move in and for Don to decide that this house was going to be his next grand achievement. The often shy, gentle and selfless Don Bodette did not speak often of his other more laudable lifetime experiences, but as our restoration efforts escalated from one or two rooms to all ten rooms over the course of the next 24 months, so did our respect for each other. I remember asking Don about The Bodette Family history and him telling me that he was the maker and keeper of the "Sacred Scrolls" that graphed out the entire geneology. "Is Tom Bodette one of your relatives?" I asked. Tom Bodette had gained fame in the 90s as the radio and TV voice for "We'll leave the light on for ya" Motel 6 commercial. Don proudly went upstairs to his bedroom and returned with what looked like one side of a Hebraic Torah. "Hold this," he suggested as he placed the roll on the floor near the west wall of the kitchen and commenced backing up while unrolling the calligraphic handwritten genealogy that was still going as he approached the dining room's east wall some 30 feet away. "Lets see, ah yes, here's Diane and me and somewhere over here, yes, here's Tom," he so humbly proclaimed. It was a sight to behold.

As the weeks and months went by, Don progressed from room to room down-stairs, then the four bedrooms and bath on the second floor the following year. Don's skills and often superhuman efforts removing layers and decades of accumulated building materials, running new electric outlets, replacing settled insulation and even restoring the original "horsehair" plaster lathe convinced me that I must not only acquire the materials he would need to achieve our goal, but too, I must step up to the plate and insist that we trade out his rent for his efforts.

As my respect for Don's work ethic and friendship grew, so did my concern for his wellbeing. He seemed to be living exclusively on cigarettes and popcorn, while not shying away from informing me that he only slept two-three hours a night. When

I told him that I wanted to get him a good quality cartridge-style respirator for the demolition phase of the project, he refused to wear one. It was as if he insisted on becoming one, organically and inextricably, with the toxic byproduct of his achievement. But why?

The same year that Linda and I made the leap away from teaching tenure and relocated to the Green Mountain National Forest of Vermont, Don Bodette ran an ad in the local paper there stating "Vietnam Veterans, we need to talk!" He had served in the Vietnam War in its early years and after being doused with "Agent Orange" for months, getting his backside riddled with shrapnel and living with pieces still lodged next to his spinal cord, he was retired with honors and a Purple Heart for bravery in 1968. But the psychological remnants of war are often more destructive and more deceptive than the physiological ones. Ten years on, Don's pain had not diminished and he needed to talk. The ad struck a nerve with Jake Jacobsen, then Bobby Muller and after several meeting in Don's living room, the chapter-based Vietnam Veterans Association was born.

So, Don Bodette was a proud Vietnam Veteran and I a proud Anti-Vietnam War protestor and pacifist, brought together in the most unlikely of places and seemingly worlds apart. How then did our friendship grow stronger within the brevity of our crossed paths? While working with Don, I spoke with blunt honesty about never having blamed the troops for the war, about its misguided purpose and about the need to stop the senseless bloodshed. It wasn't easy but over time Don came to understand the logic and patriotic necessity of the opposing viewpoint and with sweat and shared purpose Gentleman Don and I brought a piece of Colonial history, built during George Washington's Presidency, back to life.

Less than one year after his grand and final project, Don Bodette passed away on August 10, 1997. He was only 48 years young.

To this day, Don's extraordinary craftsmanship lives on at the Kingsley Grist Mill National Historic Site in East Clarendon, Vermont.

david clayton thomas
BLOOD, SWEAT, & TEARS

By 1995, Linda and I found ourselves caught up in the day to day responsibilities of renovation and maintenance at our Vermont State historic property nearby Killington and Rutland. We had been living in one level of the Kingsley Grist Mill's 94 ft. tall, six story, unfinished structure since 1980. Fifteen years into our scheduled 12 years rehabilitation project, we were barely past fixing the leaks in the 100 year-old slate roof. With 5 stories yet to address, our original 12 year completion schedule was looking more like 24.

The dog days of summer '95 were upon us when we received a call from The Mayor out in Yuma. He had been doing

some internet research and found out that David Clayton Thomas, the lead singer for Blood, Sweat & Tears was going to be appearing at a festival in upstate New York, the following week. Hunter Mountain was only a two hour drive from our home and we had not tracked down anyone to date from that group. I placed a phone call to Hunter Mountain to make sure that he was still coming, then headed down the New York Thruway back to the ubiquitously artsy Catskill Mountains.

Thomas' rise to fame as the sultry lead vocalist in an almost counter-culture Jazz/Rock American band had an extremely dubious beginning. Born David Henry Thomsett in Surrey, England, the son of a decorated World War II soldier and a piano-playing mother who met at an army hospital, David relocated early on with his family to Toronto, Canada. There he was taught music by his mom but, because of the family's paternal dysfunction, ran away from home as a teenager. According to his biography, David spent time in jail and became a juvenile delinquent until his release in 1962. Until turning 21, he picked up and practiced guitar emulating his hero John Lee Hooker. By 1967, David joined the band Phoenix and took up residency at Steve Paul's The Scene but was quickly deported by the U.S. government for working here illegally. That same year Al Kooper re-named the group Blood, Sweat & Tears (from the 1963 Johnny Cash album title) in New York but was, by '68, himself forced out, leaving the group's guitar/vocalist Steve Katz and drummer Bobby Colomby to search for a new lead singer. Steven Stills (CS&N) and Alex Chilton (The Box Tops) were among those considered but in the end the newly visa-ed Thomas got the spot and the line up made its national debut on June 18, 1968 at Café Au Go Go in Manhattan.

We arrived at Hunter Mountain in the early afternoon and went to the ticket window with the details of our mission. Several management interventions later we were back stage waiting for Clayton Thomas to show up. I could almost sense the heavy load he was carrying when he walked up. I made the introduction and when I started explaining the project he cut me short. "What is it that you want from me?"

he inquired with an inflection of distrust. "Just your signature," I shot back. "OK, but I'm getting ready to go on." "Give us 10 seconds for a picture," I requested, as I handed him the pen and Program. How he managed the big smile for precisely the right moment that the shutter opened must come from years of practice. I didn't even bother offering a T-shirt to our aloof and distant Thomas. I figured, what goes up, must come down!

Blood, Sweat & Tears program page.

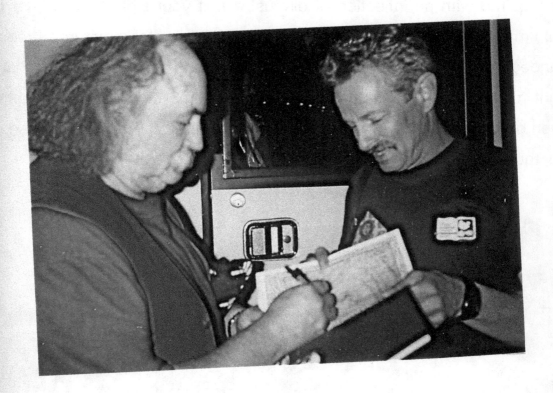

david crosby

We closed out 1995 with the amazing Carlos Santana at SPAC and had only one very difficult character to chase down the following year. The affable Graham Nash made arrangements for us to pick up comp tics and back stage passes at Will Call once again in Saratoga, New York. By '96 S.P.A.C. had become our home turf and favorite place to get together with the legends of Woodstock. Chicago was opening for the harmonic trio this night and with credentials well in hand, we sat back in the audience and enjoyed the show. "Color My World" was one of three songs Frank Simms had played so eloquently at our wedding back in '73. Occasionally in life's journey, a combination of elements and experiences converge to heighten one's appreciation and elevate one's senses. This was such a time.

During the concert, David Crosby had made an off-the-cuff remark about maybe it being time for him to stop being so "political" on stage. The gist seemed to be that no one was really listening anyway. By the time we made it back stage after the show this time, much of the mayhem had subsided but there, in the sparsely populated meet and greet room of our past, were Graham, his wife Susan and son Jackson doing their Green Peace thing. I approached Graham as if we had been childhood friends. He introduced Lin and me to his family. As much as I wanted the moment to last, I knew that we were here, after all, to try and catch up with Crosby. So I just kind of threw it out there. "Graham," I inquired, "do you know if David is still around?" Graham's response suggested that he had once again eluded our efforts, but Susan had a different plan. Her eyes widened to the challenge. She turned to me and said, "Let's see if we can catch him before his bus leaves!" Off we ran with Susan leading the charge. Down the hall and out to the bus dock where one bus remained, engine running. We stood back as Susan hammered on the door while shouting to the driver, "Is David inside?" The door swung open. "David, can you come out for a moment? The folks doing the Woodstock Project would like to meet you." And finally, there he was, the humble and reclusive David Crosby. Before I had a chance to compose my thoughts, David was already so over us. "OK, click, click. Lets get this over with," were the first words out of his mouth. How do you respond to that comment? As I readied the Program and the pen, Linda thought fast and threw it right back on David. "By the way David," she retorted, "don't ever stop speaking your mind on stage. It's your art and expression that we rely on." Linda had stopped David dead in his tracks. His eyes met hers and his whole demeanor changed. Now focused on the moment, David humbly responded, "Thank you for really listening."

I can see how, at the great distance separating the artist from the art appreciator, it is easy to lose touch; to forget the very personal nature of a message delivered in a very impersonal concert setting. Rare is the occasion one gets to break down that very imposing barrier and share an aha moment with an icon like David Crosby. David got the shirt. We all hugged and went our separate ways, feeling privileged to have met.

"Daylight again, following me to bed

I think about a hundred years ago, how my fathers bled

I think I see a valley, covered with bones in blue

All the brave soldiers that can not get older been askin' after you

Hear the past a callin', from Ar-megeddon's side

When everyone's talkin' and none is listening, how can we decide?

Find the cost of freedom, buried in the ground

Mother earth will swallow you, lay your body down."

-Stephen Stills, 1970 (Goldhill Music)

Helplessly hoping
her harlequin hovers nearby
awaiting a word
Gasping at glimpses
of gentle true spirit he runs,
wishing he could fly,
Only to trip at the sound
of good-bye.*

*Crosby, Stills & Nash

David Crosby - "Mission Accomplished",
June 25, 1996 Saratoga Performing Arts
Center, New York.

leslie west
MOUNTAIN

Leslie Weinstein learned to play guitar while growing up in Hackensack, New Jersey and Long Island. When his parents divorced he changed his surname to West and formed the R&B band The Vagrants. Several of the Vagrants albums were produced by Cream collaborator Felix Pappalardi in the late 60's when, in 1969, just months before Woodstock, the two formed Mountain. N.D. Smart (drums) and Steve Knight (keyboard) rounded out the band's lineup for their 4th live performance together on the afternoon of August 14th, at Yasgur's Farm.

We caught up to Leslie at Stratton Mountain, Vermont, and

were ushered into his dress room after the show for the Project. He was with a couple of other band members when we interrupted his post-concert indulgence. I explained what we were doing but it was clear that he just didn't really give a shit. OK, maybe I'll throw out some questions that will solicit a dialogue of his recollections and break the ice. " So, what do you remember about your famous Woodstock appearance?" I asked, hoping to start with a broad perspective and ferret out the details as we went along. West's shockingly terminal answer caught me completely off guard. Without lifting his attention from the Program he was signing, he answered "Not a fucking thing!" A second try offered no new revelations and that, my friends, was the end of that. Did you at least enjoy the T-shirt Leslie?

ravi & annoushka shankar

Ravinda Shankar, the sandskrit surname of Robindro Shaunkor Chowdhury, born April 7, 1920 in Varanasi, India, did not take well to what he saw on Friday, April 15th 1969. By the time Ravi would take the stage at Woodstock he had already mastered the four Vedic scriptures of Hinduism earning him the title of Pandit, signed a contract with Richard Bock's World Pacific Records recording studio (the recording studio of The Byrds), become the Hundustani Classical Master and mentor for George Harrison who used his sitar teachings on the 1965 Beatles album Rubber Soul single "Norwegian Wood" for the first time, won a Grammy Award for Best Chamber Music Performance in his Yehudi Menuhin collaboration of "West meets East," opened the Kinnara School of Music in Los Angeles California, published his autobiography "My Music, My Life" and was by all accounts the most celebrated Sitar artist on the planet.

Weeks before his scheduled performance at the University of Connecticut at Storrs on September 29th 1997, I sent a packet of Woodstock Program Project information to Mr. Sheldon Soffer, Ravi Shankar's east coast agent in Manhattan. A follow-up call reveals that Ravi has agreed to not only meet with us after the show but to have us as his guests for the night's performance..

The entire evening proved to be one huge cultural learning experience, starting the moment we approached the lobby of the U-Conn auditorium concert site. The auditorium doors remained closed until 30 minutes before the show-time however, as a result of the cold and drizzly weather outside, and the ticket windows and lobby were packed. Not just packed, but packed tightly. We found ourselves enveloped in the cultural dynamic of personal spacial relationships. As a kid growing up I remember my father telling me that when he was in the service, for a time in India during World War II, he had never seen so many people in one place in his life and how difficult it was for him to get used to their sense of personal space. The vast majority of attendees at the event were of middle eastern decent and seemed quite comfortable shoulder to shoulder in the lobby's confined space. Linda and I were so enamored by the elegance and visual intensity of the traditional apparel on display here that before we could become claustrophobic, the venue doors swung open.

Inside, the beauty of the fabrics and accessories worn by the crowd was enhanced by Ravi's set décor. The ushers directed us to the third row center stage guest seating where I struck up a conversation with the impeccably dressed Indian gentleman sitting to my right. I couldn't take my eyes off his glove leather light fawn shoes. "I was admiring your shoes," I said, to break the ice. The rest of his clothing was drop dead gorgeous as well, but the shoes were completely over the top. When prompted for details, he told me that he had had them custom made by one of India's most celebrated leathercraftsmen. "They cost $1,500." Had I worn a tuxedo to this show, I would have been underdressed!

The lesson continued as the show progressed. Accompanying Ravi, who, during the first half of the concert, was dressed in a breathtaking handmade Sherwani, was his longtime friend and tabla player, Alla Rakhaw. As with the rest of the troupe, Alla was dressed in a more comfortable linen Kurta style top. They were seated on a set of burgundy and blue Indian woven rugs and traditional tasseled pillows. No computerized stage light boards or laser light shows here. Simple traditional elegance and brilliant handwoven fabric gave the set a warmth and softness matched only by the artist himself. But as much as I was willingly drawn into the hypnotic resonance of Ravi's sitar, I could not for the life of me decipher the seemingly random beat or rhythm that his feet kept as he played. As hard as I tried, I could not grasp the secret. Those $1,500 shoes to my right however, were keeping perfect Ravi-time.

After intermission, Ravi proudly introduced the rising star that would accompany him for the rest of the evening. "Please welcome my daughter Anoushka." Draped in a flowing Tangail Saree, Anoushka lit up the stage with her warm smile and tempered, almost shy demeanor. But it was her mastery of the art her father taught her that brought the audience to their feet on more than one occasion this night.

Ravi sent an assistant out to greet us after the audience had left the auditorium. We were led backstage and asked to wait outside a steel grey door. Moments later the door opened revealing a dressing room filled with mostly women in traditional clothing. A single steel folding chair was brought out and placed in the hall beside the door. Ravi emerged from inside and took his seat among us. Only a half dozen people were honored to have a personal audience with the master tonight. Linda and I stayed back, hoping to be last, and just as we are about to meet Ravi as the last two in the hallway, out walked Anoushka from the dressing room to join her dad. She listened intently as I spoke to her father about the Program Project and he recounted his perspective on his Woodstock experience and his general distain for the drug-laden hippie culture. "It was a turbulent time for America," he explained. The sheer size and scope of the event was unsettling for him but time had given Ravi an insight into the ubiquity of that historic weekend and never having seen the Program, he welcomed his place among its greats.

"Permeating kharma, totally crimson vedic
tabla tree roots by life's flow
Ranjayati iti Rage.....harrisonic

Mantra restrusting force"

* verse on Ravi's Program page.
** the same year that Jazz Saxaphonist
John Coltrane named his son, born August 6, 1965, Ravi.

In memoriam, Ravi Shankar December 11, 2012

Thank you sweet, gentle man.

Ravi and daughter Annoushka Shankar outside their dressing room at UCONN's Jorgensen auditorium, September 20, 1997, Storrs, Connecticut.

JOAN BAEZ
Just Released! "David's Album" Vanguard

joan baez
PART TWO

The Rutland Herald ran an ad for Joan Baez' return to the Flynn Theater in Burlington. I placed a call to her secretary out on the west coast who contacted her road manager Crook Stewart. After the show Crook gave us the all clear to go down to the dressing rooms where we caught up with the gracious Ms. Baez once again. Joan broke away from a meeting with UVM theater students momentary to pose for a picture and accept a project T-shirt from us. This was to be the first and last time I would embrace the divine Ms. Baez. I did not keep her, although I would have loved to.

melancholy memoirs of the dead

For several years after the Grateful Dead Highgate, Vermont fiasco, Kevin of Yuma made effort upon effort to get us hooked up with the remaining members of the band, now touring under the names "Further Tour" and sometimes "The Dead."

Our first go at it was back at SPAC in 1998. Management and Security brought Linda and me backstage to the tour headquarters room just before the afternoon sound check was to commence. One advance man (actually a charming black woman) was present at the tour's computer control center in one of the many small backstage rooms.. Charlie, our security buddy, left us and returned to his post and as we shared our mission with her and were told that the person to talk to was Ken Viola, the tour manager. "He should be here any minute," she anxiously announced. This was the most encouragement we'd experienced from any member of the Dead organization...then Ken Viola arrived.

"Mr. Viola, Hi I'm Ron Evans and this is my wife Linda. We're doing the Woodstock Program Project" and that's as far as I got. "Who the fuck let this guy in here? I didn't say you could be in here. Someone call security," Ken urged. "I'm here to get permission," I retorted. "Get these people out of here now," he insisted, as if there was someone else in the room to handcuff me on the spot. Our friendly receptionist was stunned but had no other choice and neither did Charlie when he returned to the room. "You don't need to throw us out, we'll leave on our own," I insisted, "but you guys should be ashamed of yourselves for treating your fans and followers with such disdain." It was the best criticism I could muster up on the moment. Ken was not fazed. "Get this son of a bitch out of here," he shouted to Charlie. Charlie shot me an apologetic gaze and said,"I have to do what they want Ron." I was keenly aware of the legal protocol and as we retraced our steps down the famous backstage hallway, Charlie turned to me and said, "These guys are such ass-holes, this isn't the first time," he boasted. Lin and I packed up and headed home after strike two.

We would make one final attempt with The Dead the following summer when the Mayor flew back home and convinced us to give it a go. We agreed but made it clear that we were doing it for him and not the dead. Kevin purchased the tickets. We left Kevin in the pre-concert vendor crowd and headed backstage where we ran smack into Dennis McNally who must have had our identities committed to memory by now. "If I see you two within 50 feet of the backstage entrance, I will call the police," he threatened. OK, game over. We rejoined Kevin at the vendor tents and as we began recounting our complete frustration with the blatantly hateful treatment we had experienced at the hands of the Dead's management and publicist, Kevin's eyes widened and with the shyest of gestures he began gesturing with his index finger for us to turn around. "What?" I asked. "Right behind you Ron, it's Bob Weir." I turned and saw a couple directly behind me stopped in a golf cart. "Are you sure?" I asked Kevin naively. He looked at me like "Duh." If anyone knew Bob Weir it was he. I spun around, introduced myself, mentioned the Woodstock Project and told Bob that it would be an honor to have his participation. OK, even I didn't see this one coming! "Who do you think I am?" he asked. "Do you think I'm Bob Weir?" I glanced over at Kevin who rolled his eyes in disbelief. "Yes, I do," was my challenge. "You're mistaking me for someone else," he concluded. "If I was Bob Weir, would I be driving a golf cart?" he suggested with a shit eating grin on his face, and sped off.

STRIKE THREE!

paving paradise
PUTTING UP A PARKING LOT

Remember Allen Gerry? Well, in 1997 Gerry's foundation purchased the 600-acre farm site of the Woodstock Festival plus 1,400 additional acres around the farm with the long term plan of constructing home sites and condominiums about the perimeter of a Bethel Woods Concert Center and "Woodstock Museum." Our billionaire hippie hater who wanted nothing to do with the historic 1969 event now owned it all. And like most hyper-wealthy corporate executives, Gerry was in it for the money alone.

Recollections of our emotional and depressing experience at the 1999, 30th Anniversary at Yasgur's Farm have been so badly repressed by me that I needed to ask Linda to help put this timeline together. Here are her recollections:

I remember approaching The Garden on the same town road we had traveled the very first time we came to this magical place. Back then, the car stopped and Ron said, "This is it." We walked the sun-drenched cornfield and hillside in peace and found comfort in knowing what had taken place on this very spot. It seemed so right that it should remain a people's place. That was, after all, the essence of the whole Woodstock legacy.

Well this time through we never even made it to that spot. As we approached the last intersection on West Shore Road, we observed a sawhorse like barricade and a police car parked adjacent to it on the opposite side of the intersection. Since we had been traveling for hours, Ron decided to park on the side of the road, stretch his legs and walk over to the police officer to explain our Project. As he began walking toward the cruiser, a very young looking policeman emerged, put his right hand on his gun and shouted, "Sir, get back in your vehicle!" Ron put his hands in the air and said, "Hold on, I just wanted to ask you a few questions." "I'll speak to you when you get back in your car," the officer insisted. OK. What's this all about, I wondered. Where's "Officer Friendly" when you need him?

Once again in the driver's seat, Ron began explaining the reason for our visit to the curt, brusk and inexperienced policeman. "Officer Un-friendly" wasn't the slightest bit interested in what we were doing and insisted that we immediately turn around and go back to White Lake, pick up the highway and approach Hurd Road from there. Yes, the times they were a'changing and along with them, the tone of authority. We weren't off to a good start.

Entering the site's main gate was a heartwrenching experience. No longer able to ascend the hill and enjoy the vista overlooking Woodstock's natural amphitheater, we were instead led into a series of picket fenced parking lots, each named after a flower and identified with standardized yellow and blue graphic signage. We parked in "Daisy" or "Daffodil" or who cares and entered through the gates patrolled by more police and Gerry employees dressed in uniforms, complete with baseball caps, that matched the location finder flower signage in the lots.

Linda's recall still sends chills down my spine. "The grounds were cordoned off for vendors in one spot, eating in another nearby and an elaborate stage erected at the site of the original. The property was surrounded by page fencing and security but for the price of admission you got to enjoy Gerry's gardens of tulip bulbs and bordered landscape mulch. To add insult to psychological injury, Reba Macintyre, a country and western recording artist, was on stage bragging about her many successes and what a fabulous person she was. That was it. We couldn't take it anymore. In less than a year and a half, Gerry had already made a complete mockery of Woodstock's humble and principled beginnings. Yasgur's Dairy Farm was well on its way to being pasteurized, homogenized and reconstituted. We left, determined to get more answers. After meeting up with Duke Devlin and yes, the real Officer Friendly, outside the gates on Hurd, we traveled back down the highway to White Lake village and dropped in on Debbie Fallon, the director of the Bethel/Woodstock Museum There were no security guards, police cruisers or bogus flower power signs here. Ron asked Debbie to sign the official program and gave her a t-shirt to display in her modest but heartwarming little museum."

john sebastian
A LOVIN' SPOONFUL

We headed home with a profound sense that our nation was going down the wrong path to peace and prosperity and found little to celebrate in the first five years of the new millennium. Media pundits had every PC owner tied up in knots over Y2K, prognosticators guaranteed the end of the world, again. W. took the oath of office and then came 9/11. Until John Fogerty came to Look Park outside North Hampton, Massachusetts in 2005, we had only one other occasion to pursue a fleeting opportunity with the Lovin' Spoonful's lead vocalist, John B. Sebastian.

In the fall of 2002, John played a small venue at the historic Sturbridge Village in north central Massachusetts. I simply called the venue and management there told me that they would let John know of our intentions. It was suggested that we arrive early. Fifteen minutes after we set up for him backstage, John walked in alone. We sat down and talked.

John had grown up in and around music. His father was a classical harmonica player and his mother a radio script writer in Greenwich Village, New York. John's grandmother, Vivian Vance (Ethel Mertz), was the very famous co-star of TV's #1 sit-com "I Love Lucy."

John played Woodstock on the 2nd day of the concert, squeezing in 5 songs between Country Joe McDonald and Santana. He talked to Lin and me about going out on stage after smoking grass backstage. He was soft spoken but a bit distracted as he signed the first bond page of the Program and accepted our T-shirt as a gift of thanks. We joined the small but enthusiastic crowd for the show. John did not disappoint.

John Sebastian and Friends, backstage before the show, October 12, 2002. Sturbridge Village, Massachusetts.

john fogerty & family

As the dot.com bubble morphed into an avarice pseudo real estate "grab and flip," Linda and I tried to stay focused on the long term goals of completing our 12 year, turned 24 year, restoration of the Kingsley Grist Mill Historic Site and subsequently applying to the United States Department of Interior for National Historic status. Knowing, too, that none of us were getting any younger, we made some graphic modifications to our first T-shirt concept, printed up some new improved promotional sheets for "The Original Woodstock Program Project" and hit the road for our second and perhaps final chance to get together with the renowned gravel voiced lead singer/

songwriter extraordinaire Mr. John Fogerty.

Seven years earlier, on July 5th, 1998 we were off stage left with John's road manager minutes before the start of his "Premonition Tour" concert at the Saratoga Performing Arts Center when, with disappointment in his voice, he explained to us that John did his meet and greets before, not after, his events. "After the show, he goes back to be with his family and friends," we're told. Then, "Wait here a moment." Bob broke away, walked over to center stage where John was setting up, guitar in hand, had a few words, then returned to us with a suggestion which I would never hear again in my 25 years of chasing Woodstock. "John said if you're going to be around tomorrow morning, he would like to invite you to stop by his hotel room to do your project there!" Wow, what a generous offer. We were stunned. Then it dawned on me. "Please thank him for us but we have an appointment in Vermont tomorrow morning that we must keep" I replied apologetically. "Can we take a rain check?" I joked, whilst dying inside. As the director of Centre Sport Health Club back home, Linda had to open at 6 am. She had never let her members down and at the time, we were so broke that a Saratoga hotel room was out of the question. We thanked Bob and descended the stairs of the bus platform there for the very last time. Driving home I couldn't help but wonder if I would live to regret the conundrum.

June 4th, 2005 brought picture perfect summer weather to central Massachusetts. We decided to make a day of it. "Look" is one of those 19th century, old New England neighborhood parks that exude charm and elegance. Dedicated in 1930, the 150-acre oasis was given to the city of Florence by a 19th century brush manufacturer named Frank Newhall Look. Today, Look Park offered picnic and cookout grills for simply relaxing with the family or if exhaustion suits you better, a full day of pedal boating, tennis, miniature golf, hiking, steam train riding and petting zoo followed by an evening concert at the Pines Theater should fit the bill.

After lunch in Northampton next door, Lin and I checked in with John's tour manager early and were told to wait at the service road entrance to the concert site after the ticket holders were let into the theater. Moments later John, his wife Julie and their 5 year old daughter Kelsy Cameron cruised out from back stage in a sleek and silent electric golf cart (as in Bob Weir) and pulled up along side us for the moment we had thought we'd let slip by. Our few minutes together showed me the kind of people John and Julie Fogerty are. They had never seen the Woodstock Program before and enjoyed sharing the moment with daughter Kelsy. As we shook hands and extended our thanks and warmest regards, I too had a premonition that someday I would get to have my picture taken with John and his famous Woodstock amplifier. What do you say Julie and Kelsy, would that be OK?

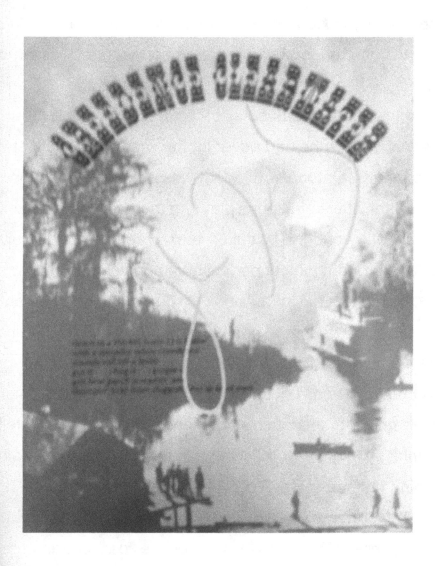

jocko & donny
SHA-NA-NA

Thirty six years beyond their auspicious Woodstock performance, Donny York and Jocko, aka Sha-Na-Na, were still wowing audiences when Linda and I caught up with them outside of Boston. As you can see from the photos, these two still know how to have fun. They had never seen the Original Woodstock Program and after spending some time paging through it, seemed honored to be part of its history. Thanks guys. The honor was ours. I hope you've worn the shirts?

elliott landy
LANDYVISION

Only two years before Woodstock, Elliott had begun making a name for himself in the world of counter-culture photography by documenting the anti-Vietnam War protests and the rise to stardom of Janis Joplin, Jimi Hendrix and Jim Morrison. In the decade to follow, his work would grace the covers of Rolling Stone, LIFE and The Saturday Evening Post and his portrait photos the album covers of Bob Dylan's "Nashville Skyline," Van Morrison's 'Moondance" and The Band's eponymous second album "The Band."

We caught up with Elliott, or should I say we caught up with each other, less than a half hour from our home in Vermont. My wife Linda had begun volunteering and exhibiting at the prestigious Manchester, Vermont Southern Vermont Art Center campus when it was announced that Mr. Landy would be doing a presentation in the Arkell Pavillion followed by a book signing at the newly constructed Wilson Museum.

Elliott's presentation covered most of his early black and white photo work culminating with Woodstock. When we made our way over to the museum afterward we found him wrapped in conversation with someone familiar. As we approached, we discovered it was Landy doing the interviewing and taping of our old friend, professional psyciatrist, Al Coglan. We took up seats across the lobby from the two and listened intently as Al revealed to Elliott that he had been one of the volunteers who helped staff the medical emergency tent, known at the time as the "Freakout" tent, at Woodstock on the weekend of August 15, 16 and 17, 1969. Lin and I had come to know Al and his wife when, back in the 80's, we were designing and setting up health clubs in central Vermont and henceforward, creating and piloting the advanced arthritis aquatics exercise program for The Arthritis Foundation of America. As active club members, the Coglan's never brought up the Woodstock connection and somehow, neither did we. Here then we celebrated the common values and causes that brought us together, again, for this serendipitous first time.

Al glanced across the glass foyer lobby of the Wilson Gallery, the epicenter of the Southern Vermont Art Center's expansive campus of rolling hills and sculpted pastures. We acknowledged each other briefly as Elliott leaned the microphone closer in his direction. "I spent most of that weekend backstage helping O.D.s and Bad Trips get their feet back on the ground," Al lamented. "It was a once in a lifetime experience." At the conclusion of the interview Al and I agreed to catch up on the Woodstock Program Project at his office in Rutland at a later date.

Elliott Landy had travelled from his Woodstock home to Vermont with partner Lynda, a beautiful brunette with a radiant smile and a keen eye for detail. As Elliott helped me unpack the Woodstock program and accompanying Landy poster, Lynda prepared her video camera and Linda her digital camera. On August 13th, 2005 another Woodstock legend chased down.

Update: 8 years after our Vermont meet-up, I decided to try to make contact with Elliott and Lynda once again. We were on a return trip home passing Woodstock on the New York State Thruway when we got the news that the Landys were entertaining family and friends from out of town and didn't have much free time. "Give me a call on my cell when you get into town and we'll see what we can do," Elliott suggested. By the time he received my response, Lin and I had already stopped for an amazing lunch at Bread Alone Bakery. We pulled up a couple of window bar seats not far from the entrance. Linda rolled her eyes and gestured toward the wall above us. We had landed directly beneath a signed, framed original Elliott Landy "Nashville Skyline" color photograph. There was Bob Dylan's mug staring right at us when the phone rang. It was the artist himself inviting us to join him at another garden cafe venue just up the road. When I told him where we were he laughed. "We go there almost every morning but today needed more space and quiet to visit with my sister and friends. Stop by." We hopped in the car and instead of going up the road, we went down the road. We were six miles south of Woodstock when we discovered that the cafe we were looking for was actually one mile NORTH of Woodstock. Crap. Topping out at 60 mph in a 45 zone, I turned to Linda and said the first thing that popped into my head – "I guess we're STILL chasing Woodstock!"

It was a picture perfect autumn afternoon as we pulled into the Suncross Cafe's pumpkin-adourned outdoor garden dining area. Elliott and Lynda invited us to join they and their guests under a sun drenched pergola as we caught up on the program and where it had taken us since we last met. Our rescued greyhounds Tully Fullers and Emilee made the rounds getting pets from everyone seated at the black steel mesh patio table. These soulful quadrupeds can win over even the toughest crowd; one look into their chestnut eyes and these guys were jello. The conversation flowed freely around the table as we reminisced about our first meet up in Vermont and discussed plans for future program project participants. Elliott and Lynda made it clear that this chase was far from over.

Finally, my interest was in asking Elliott's advice about the use of one his legendary photos of The Band at Big Pink for this manuscript. He was honest and sincere as he explained the procedures of licensing their use through his agent, supplying me with that contact information if I chose that route. Then he told me something about copyright law that I will never forget. We hugged and headed home.

The Bands legendary Big Pink house album photo in 1968 and today in a rare south side photo showing the new roof dormer addition. Bob Dylan and The Band wrote and recorded the salient Basement Tapes (1975) and The Band wrote most of their first album here.

trump gets "fired"

Shortly after 9/11 Linda and I began making the necessary modifications to our lifestyle so that we could spend a few months every winter in a warmer part of the country. The logic was that if we could completely shut down our Grist Mill for January, February and March, the money we would save on heat and electric, i.e. the smaller carbon foot print, would virtually pay for the entire trip. Furthermore, by 2003 Linda had reached an impasse with having put aside, for 25 years, the creativity she had exhibited as a child and had mastered as a student and young adult. She needed a muse for her return to 2-D Design Art.

Our 2002 December departure from snowbound Vermont, destination Phoenix, Arizona, was quite a sight to behold. Linda had managed to pack three months worth of clothing and artist supplies plus two full grown greyhounds and two almost mature adults into a 55 mile per gallon 1994 Geo Metro hatch back for the 3,000 mile, six-day journey. Of all the classic cars we have owned and restored since 1972, this little three cylinder wonder was always her favorite and it never let us down.

We checked into a small daily motel and set out to find accommodations for the long winter stay, ending up at an economical new extended stay hotel at the base of Squaw Peak in north Phoenix. It was time to drop in on cousins Peter and Jesse with the news that we were in town for the winter and the hope that, even though we had only met once or twice before, our common interests would bring us together. From the moment we arrived at their famous desert sand white and process-blue curvilinear Blaine Drake home off Camelback, the four of us were inseparable. We seemed to connect on almost every moral, ethical and philosophical level of interest, spending countless days and evenings embroiled in world events and shared solutions. The winters of '02 and '03 vanished amidst the eclectic environment and sometimes eccentric behavior that perhaps we all displayed at times.

With family in Tampa and our beloved greyhound Nubi diagnosed with bone cancer, we chose Bonita Springs, Florida for the subsequent two winter seasons. Arrangements at another extended stay hotel there proved easy. Design images began flowing through Linda's brain faster than she could record them and even I made a preliminary attempt at writing my first book on exercise, but the geologic desert diversity and the Wrightian architecture of the southwest proved too compelling to ignore. By January of 2005 we were back in Phoenix with the offer to stay in the guest cottage of Peter and Jesse's famous Wright/Drake home nearby the Arizona Biltmore. That's when things got interesting.

Both of Peter's parents were close Frank Lloyd Wright associates, father Blaine having relocated from Wisconsin to Phoenix, after the Second World War, with the construction of Wright's "Taliesin West" home and school north of Scottsdale and mother Hulda joining him there and contributing to Wright's legacy by creating many of the original architectural design and landscape renderings, including the prominent sketches and color concept drawings of Wright's most famous residence, Fallingwater.

2006 marked the first of two consecutive winters that Peter and Jesse offered to let us "crash" in the curved block two car garage, turned quasi-finished guest house, we all referred to as the "Cassita." The sun-drenched Sonoran tangerine tree in early season bloom outside our humble retreat's front door supplied us with daily just-picked morning succulence and the indigenous jack rabbit population kept our female greyhound Nyla entertained by scampering into the hedgerows of Oleander circumscribing the two-acre lot when she rushed into the center of their "briar patch" to do her business. "So, Peter what have been up to while we've been away," I inquired. "The Donald," was his answer.

As if he didn't own enough real estate, New York developer Donald Trump decided that the Camelback corridor between 22nd Street and 24th Street needed a Trump tower. So in 2004 he submitted a proposal to build a condo and hotel tower directly across from the two story Biltmore Hotel and Fashion Plaza, the most valuable block of land in all of Arizona. Trump knew going in that the zoning requirements for his project limited the building height to 56 feet, but, after all he was The Donald and, in his world, rules are meant to be altered. So Trump's egomaniacal plan called for a 550,000 sq. ft., 190' tall monolith that would virtually eliminate every other desert valley vista in northeast Phoenix.

To accomplish the task of re-writing the law to suit his needs, Trump put his best man on the job, 28 year-old Trump Jr. But what the Donalds collectively failed to account for in their master plan to "Conquer Camelback" was the presence of one contemplative Harvard grad in his subterranean Frank Lloyd Wright red concrete command center only two blocks away. In less than three months, Peter and his next door neighbor Jeff Fine formed the Stop Trump Movement, collected over 19,000 signatures, engaged the "Help me get Trump out of my back yard" slogan and forced The Trumps into a referendum battle they had little hope of winning. By March 2, 2005 only two of the Phoenix City Council's five-member sub-committee had swung over to Trump's side and on December 21st, just weeks before our arrival, Donald and Donald Jr. "officially" withdrew their un-official proposal. Peter had done something that the rest of America could only dream of doing: metaphorically looked Trump right in the eye and said, "You're fired." It was going to be another great winter in Paradise!

While pursuing excellence from his concrete bunker, Peter noticed that Janis Joplin's brother and sister were going to be dropping in at the Rock Star Gallery in nearby Scottsdale. I figured that, even though I had left the Original Woodstock Program back in Vermont, it would only be right to spend some time with the siblings of the icon I had been so intimate with. So off we went.

Joplin siblings Michael and Laura were already into their big sister presentation when we arrived.. Surrounded by lite-line and ocassional sepia/ monotone prints of Joplin originals, younger sister Laura was describing to the packed house how as kids growing up in Port Arthur, Texas she and Michael were not as aware of the music side of Janis' life as they were the fun loving, artistic and caring big sister role she willingly accepted. "She read me bedtime stories as a kid and we did a lot of girly stuff together" admitted Laura. Dressing up with boas in their hair and putting on jewelry was a vivid memory for her.

For Michael, who is four years younger yet, it was more about seeing his big sister on national TV for the first time and recalling the family's first trip out to San Francisco. "It was the Summer of Love, 1967. The family wanted to see how Janis was getting along. I remember driving around Haight Ashbury looking at all the hippies and realizing how insular our Texas homelife was," Michael recalled.

Laura closed out the talk with a description of Janis' pen and ink prints being offered for sale.   Most were done by Janis in her high school years and shortly thereafter. They are deliberate, minimalist, lite-line and very Oz like. I was convinced that her years of reading bedtime stories to sister Laura had toyed with Janis' mind. She became entranced by the fantasy and we by hers.

In the end Laura, Michael, Linda and I agreed to regroup with the Program to have them sign in honor of our Janis. Thanks M&L. Let's do this soon.

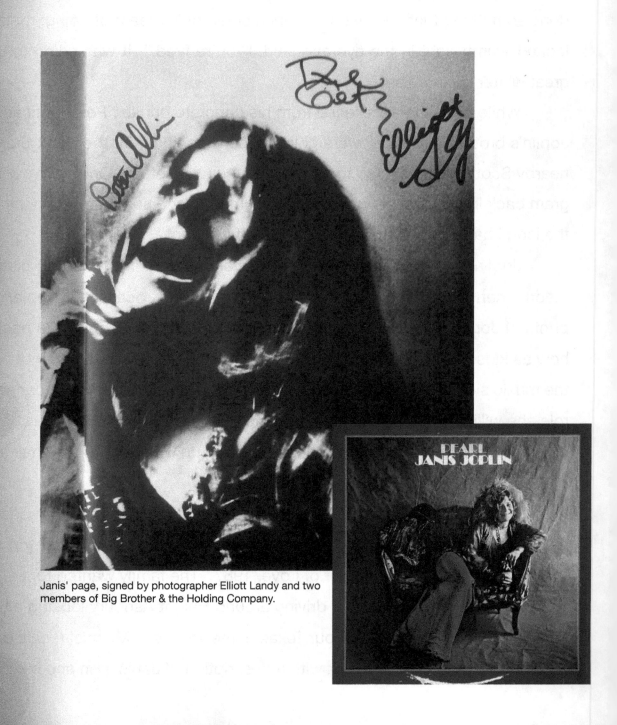

Janis' page, signed by photographer Elliott Landy and two members of Big Brother & the Holding Company.

Left to right, Chick Churchill, Leo Lyons
and Rick Lee

ten years after

The 60's British Rock Band, Ten Years After, made the final cut into the Woodstock Movie and soundtrack release of 1970. Alvin Lee (lead guitar and vocals) and Leo Lyons (bassist) had formed the band in 1966, exactly ten years after Elvis Presley had the most successful year of his career. The Nottingham U.K. band exploded onto the U.S. scene following their appearance at Yasgur's Farm on the evening of day three, Sunday August 17th.

By the summer of 2006, Alvin Lee had long split from his original Woodstock band members and was spending his time booking tour dates in and around his native Britain. I had waited a long time for Ten Years After to come back to the States, so when The Mayor called and said that they were coming to The Egg, Rockefeller Plaza in Albany, New York for a free concert, we agreed to meet up there. During the afternoon sound check, I met up with Chick Churchill, the band's keyboardist and he agreed to set us up with after show access. We hung out in the crowd knowing we were "in," but by the time the show was over, our connection had suffered a short term memory lapse and we were once again stuck on the wrong side of the fence with security insisting we stand down. I wasn't going to let this one slip away. Amidst the clamour and after show backstage frenzy, I called bass player Leo Lyons over to the security fence and basically read him the riot act. "Leo," I pronounced, "this is the only original Woodstock Program on the planet that has been photographed and signed by almost all the artists that performed that weekend and if you don't let me in to give you guys the Project T-shirts and get the photo op, it may never happen!" "Hold on," Leo reconsidered, "come over here to the gate." We were in. Check out the smiles in the pictures. It never fails to amaze me how much everyone loves the shirts.

Author's note: Wednesday, March 6, 2013. I have taken a break from writing this account and have tuned into WMNF Radio in Tampa, Florida when the announcement came over the newscast that Alvin Lee, lead guitarist and singer for Ten Years After, has died in his native England. It was always my hope to travel back to Britain soon to introduce both Alvin and his UK counterparts, The Incredible String Band, to their Woodstock Program legacy.

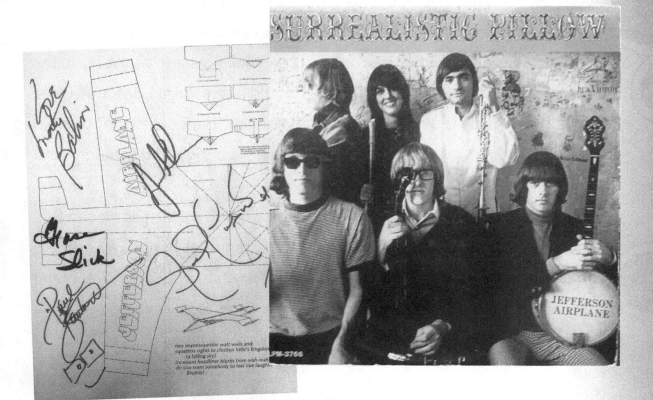

Grace Slick
JEFFERSON AIRPLANE

If you were a young man growing up in the psychedelic 60's and found homage in the Haight/Ashbury counter-culture peace movement, Grace Slick was the Queen of Hearts. The former model with the sultry voice lured you down the rabbit hole with her mindbending lyrics and free spirit. She was my impossible dream.

In years past, I had written her personally at her Malibu, California home with the hope that if we flew to the west coast to see friends, she might offer to let us pay her a visit. The iconic Grace had stopped touring with her Jefferson Airplane co-stars and had more recently given her time to her visual fine arts and pet adoption charities. It would be the symbiotic dream of a lifetime. Linda, too had returned to her design art passion, now finding eloquence in the greyhound morphology and raising money for the adoption of ex-racers while, having done my Project with all the other members of "Airplane," I would not rest until Grace's signature took its place alongside the others on the spectacular "paper airplane" graphic page created for Woodstock. I never knew if my letters were getting through but I never heard back.

Then suddenly there she was. I don't recall how I found out but someone told me that Grace was coming east for a one time appearance at the Wentworth Art Gallery in the upscale Short Hills Mall. I called the gallery and was given the name of Scott Hann, the agent that represented Ms. Slick's work. Scott owned Area Arts out of Santa Rosa, California and would be the person to contact, I was told, for arrangements.

"Grace does not sign Rock and Roll memorabilia during her art tours but if you buy a piece of Grace's work she will be more than happy to sign it for you," Scott explained, during our brief phone conversation. As much as I adored many of her whimsical images, I told him that they were out of my price range, but Scott was having none of it. Adding that I would be coming with some friends who might be interested in buying, we agreed to meet there and play it by ear.

On the phone, the staff at Wentworth Gallery were fabulous. I sent them off a promotional package for the Woodstock Project and they got back to me with a rundown of the afternoon and evening schedule for Grace Slick's exclusive appearance there. The gallery would open to the public at it's usual time for previewing but would, at 3 pm, close its doors to everyone except those collectors who had pre-purchased Ms. Slick's art. Grace would then meet with those buyers individually, posing for pictures and personalizing her work. Upon her departure at 5 pm, the gallery would once again be open to the public.

We arrived at the second level mall gallery with our former teacher friends

Warren and Amy shortly after 1 pm, anxious to meet the staff, including Mary Anne and Susan who had been so helpful on the phone. After seeing the Woodstock Program in person they were so excited to see this thing through that they kept signaling us every time something important was about to happen, first introducing us to Scott Hann, then alerting us to Ms. Slick's every move in the gallery's back office. It was very cute. Still, I was so close I couldn't let this moment slip away. But Scott was not budging. He wanted the sale and I didn't have the dough. One of us was going to have to cave; Unless!

As 3pm neared, the "Gallery Girls" gave me the sign to stick around. The glass mall doors slid shut with Warren and Amy outside and Lin and I within, and one step closer to Grace. We were now among a dozen pre-buy collectors who had shelled out thousands of dollars to own a piece of Rock Art history and to meet the legend in person. But I had dibs on the only folding chair in the room that was set up next to the only table in the room when The Queen of Hearts herself emerged from the back door of the gallery, walked over and sat down next to me, alone.

As the rest of the collectors waited patiently up front for the OK to meet Grace, I took up my role as "insider guy who was just shootin' the shit with Grace Slick while the gallery folk got things set up for the collectors." Concealing my star-struck heart rate, I introduced myself and opened up the floor to a subject in which I felt we would both have interest, renewable energy.

Eight uninterrupted minutes later, there I sat, one on one with the hippie chick of my dreams, killin' time and solving the nation's problems discussing electric cars, wind and geothermal, the oil industry and holding my own (I mean, in the conversation) when Scott walked up and informed me that it was time for Grace to start meeting her collectors. I relinquish my seat wholeheartedly knowing that the prized signature had still eluded me, yet grateful for time spent alone.

I focused my attention on Grace's agent Scott to give me just 60 seconds after everyone had finished, to do the Woodstock thing, but he grew more resistant over time. To be honest with you, I questioned whether Grace would even consent to including her signature with those of her former band members. I was missing something here and seemed at an impasse when one of the gallery assistants introduced me to the gallery director Robert Quinn. Robert understood the historic significance of the Project and unbeknownst to me, held the financial and political trump card in the game of access.

Scott relinquished his obstructionist attitude just long enough for one last moment with Grace before returning to her hotel. I opened the program. Grace scanned the signatures of her fellow band members scattered about the line drawing of a paper airplane. She hesitated momentarily as Linda fiddled unsucessfully with her new digital camera to get the flash to work and I wondered if this was going to be another one of those Johnny Winter moments. Without so much as a smile or a glance, the venerable Grace Slick reached to her right, commandeered a sharpy pen and signed her name, perhaps intentionally, on the tail of the plane between Paul Kantner and Marty Balin. Ms. Slick arose, walked slowly back to the gallery office and was gone. For one unforgettable moment I got to slip down the rabbit hole with Alice and feed my head..It was Wonder-lust.

My elusive silver haired Queen of Hearts, Grace Slick, the Wentworth Art Gallery, Short Hills, New Jersey. October 21, 2006

Left, Lee Dorman

Right, Ron Bushey

iron butterfly

On May 27th, 1968 Doug Ingle, Lee Dorman, Ron Bushey and Erik Braun arrived at Ultrasonic Recording Studio in Hempstead, Long Island to record a single that lead singer and keyboard player Ingle had recently penned. While waiting for the producer to arrive, the band sound-checked the piece, unaware that the studio engineer was actually recording them. It was this pre-recorded tape that ended up being used in the final release of Iron Butterfly's and arguably, Rock and Roll's, most famous 17 minutes.

The following year, Woodstock Ventures' Michael Lang and Artie Kornfeld booked Iron Butterfly to play at Yasgur's Farm on Sunday, August17th, at the peak of their fame and second album release. This is where things get interesting.

The band had flown to New York City and was waiting for word from Woodstock promoter Lang concerning transportation and appearance schedule. According to Lang, Iron Butterfly's road manager was arrogant and demanded that his group be picked up in Manhattan, flown to the concert site where they would "immediately" take the stage, get back in the chopper and be flown back to New York. "The decision to 'can' Butterfly was easy to make considering that, by Sunday we were already running well behind schedule and their manager was being a real asshole on the phone," I recall Michael telling me. According to Wikipedia, Ron Bushey, the group's very personable drummer, went down to the New York Port Authority Heli-port at least three times looking for the flight that never came. He must have been crestfallen.

When I started the Woodstock Program Project back in '84, I set out on a personal quest to chase down all the original artists that "played or were scheduled to play" on that historic weekend. Gig or no gig, Iron Butterfly was in the Program and deserved their place in the Woodstock legacy. When I found out that they had booked one appearance on the east coast, Linda and I made the trek to West Reading, Pennsylvania, leaving Vermont at dawn on the morning of October 6th 2006 and arriving at the Scottish Rite Cathedral Concert Hall in early afternoon.

If I had learned anything from the years doing the Woodstock Project it was that making the pre-event connections and contacts was crucial to access, but there were never any guarantees and Iron Butterfly was no exception. Calls to D.J. Production's "Terry Sr.," the shows promoter and sponsor, turned out to be a case in point. Terry knew we were coming but upon our arrival seemed to be playing it cool. Showing him the Program and explaining the historic significance of the project was met with a lukewarm reception. If we were not buying tickets, we'd have to stay out in the lobby of the auditorium during the show. Lin and I were fine with that since Terry assured us that, after the show, the band would be coming out to the lobby to sign autographs and sell their CDs. With windows in the lobby doors facing the stage, we could, if so inclined, watch the concert from there. But we trusted our host to help see this through and chose to chill out on the lobby's cushy bench seats until, near the conclusion of the concert, we heard those famous first keyboard notes followed by Lee Dorman's legendary bass rift. Butterfly had begun a 25 minute performance of the title song of Atlantic Records first album to go Platinum, the mantra of a generation, the classic psychedelic soliloquy written by Ingles as "In the Garden of Eden," but slurred by it's writer while under the influence of practically everything and therefore pronounced "In-A-Godda-Da-Vida."

"Terry Sr." consented to let us go into the concert hall for the big finale, "As long as we didn't sit down" and of course came back out at its conclusion. What a guy. Remember the 15 minute rule? Back out in the lobby, no signing, no table, no Iron Butterfly. I asked Linda to go into the concert hall and see what was going on. By now Terry was relishing his obstructionism and counting his take. "Hurry up Ron," Linda insisted. "They're getting ready to leave." We hurried down to the stage, climbed the stairs to the dressing room and met up with Ron Bushy. Ron and the rest of the tour had no idea that we were in the house and were literally smitten by the fact that we had traveled from Vermont to share the Woodstock Program with them. The moment seemed enriching for all of us until I realized that Lee Dorman was no where to be found. "I think he's left for the hotel," Ron added and as we scoured the back stage for a tall guy dressed in a black leather jacket we caught a glimpse of him heading for the stage door. Lee was not in the mood to schmooze. We handed him a pen and a T-shirt simultaneously and upon adding his John Hancock to the Butterfly page, he stepped aside and off he went. But what's really cool is that Drummer "Ron" remembered Woodstock guy "Ron" a short time later when, out in the lamp post-lit empty parking lot of the Scottish Cathedral, we tossed a football around for a few minutes and wished each other well. Iron Butterfly's world famous drummer hopped into his friend's black Camaro and drove off waving and calling me by name. How about them apples, Terry Sr.!

The blow your mind Iron Butterfly page of the Woodstock program.

the who

The first thought I ever had of doing something special with the gift my parents had bestowed upon me back on August 19, 1969 was when I was paging through the local newspaper just two years after acquiring the abandoned and dilapidated Kingsley Grist Mill property in Vermont and seeing a small filler piece touting The Who's choice of the nearby Glens Falls Civic Center as their practice site for their upcoming 1982 "It's Hard" tour. I remember thinking maybe I should drag out the Woodstock Program and make the 45 minute drive to see if there would be any chance of having them sign it. They were the bomb, they were the top, they were "The Who" and they were sooo close-by. But we were sooo broke and working sooo hard to save a piece of Vermont history before it collapsed from 45 years of neglect that we just never made the trip.

Then came the news on July 27th 2002 that the group's bassist and four de-cade- long member, John Entwistle, had died of an apparent cocaine overdose in his sleep at the Hard Rock Hotel in Vegas on the night before his opening tour date. I know it sounds selfish, but I couldn't help beating myself silly for having missed the opportunity back in '82. So, which cliché applies here: "Good things happen to those who wait" or "Things happen for a reason" or "Better late than never." As you'll see, perhaps all three.

Once again, brother Ken gets the nod for doing the web search and finding out that Roger Daltrey and Pete Townshend had squeezed in a stop at Mohegan Sun, by now a familiar venue for us, on December 1st 2006. Armed with a single contact name, we decided to make this one a cold call (Don't ask me what I was thinking).

Management at Mohegan Sun Casino was exemplary. We arrived in early af-ternoon while the doors to the venue were still open. Security inside contacted venue management. Management asked if the band was expecting us or if we were on the guest list. "No, but we have a contact name to pass on to the band if you would," I requested. We left our cell phone number and promotional packet and went to have lunch while she worked on arrangements for us. Two hours later, comp show tickets were waiting at Will Call just minutes before Chrissie Hynde and the Pretenders took the stage as the opening act.

The Mohegan Sun Arena is sized perfectly for large stadium feel and sound, yet with a capacity of about 7,500 it offers a closer and more intimate vantage point of the performance. We watched the Pretenders from our seats located midway up the stadium seating configuration and, at the break, I grabbed the Program and headed down to the stage to check in with the tour, leaving Linda behind with the camera and our belongings.

As the stage crew worked to reset for The Who, I approached the security guard who was alone at the stage left barricade. This time I was completely stone-walled. I had a name from security. I had a name from management. But this guy wasn't budging. He needed a name from the band itself and Roger Daltrey didn't qualify. "Sorry, no pass, no name, no access." As I turned to head back to the bleachers, I caught a glimpse of a tour badge around the neck of a man exiting the very security checkpoint I had just walked away from. I hurried back. "Excuse me, are you with the tour?" I asked. "Yes." Extending my hand I introduced myself, explained the purpose of my visit and asked if he was the right person to speak to about seeing Roger and Pete. He told me that he knew we were here and that he could help; however, because The Who were only minutes away from taking the stage, he would have to take it back stage for us, get it signed and bring it back. "I'm the manager for the tour." Reassuring me, "My name is Kevin." I thanked him for the very generous offer but after explaining what happened the last and only other time I let the Program out of my sight, I told him that I would have to graciously decline. I shook his hand and with profound disappointment turned to go back to Linda. Then Kevin uttered those magic words that, by now, I hope you feel as deeply as I: "Wait a moment Ron, come with me!" Pivoting around I exited the venue seating and walked with Kevin past security, past the rear of the stage, through a cavernous hallway intersection and into an office devoid of everything except two chairs and one lonely laptop.

Kevin reached over to his laptop printer and pulled out a piece of paper with some 20 to 25 bold lettered titles listed on it. Kevin handed the concert playlist to me and said, "Pete and Roger are just two doors away getting ready. If you'll trust me, I'll take the Program to them and make sure it comes right back." My trust had grown stronger. I agreed and off he went returning in what seemed like seconds. "OK, they have it and I'll make sure it's brought right back," he assured as we got into talking about the unfortunate lack of time needed to do the Project correctly including pictures, interview and T-shirts. He asked me if we were going to be available for a subsequent tour date, when it dawned on me that we were heading out to Phoenix for the next three months. Kevin punched in Phoenix, Arizona on his laptop and up popped February 28th, 2007 at the U.S. Airways Center. "Let's do it," he said. "You'll be our guests." He pulled out a business card and wrote down several cell phone numbers while suggesting that I call him a week or so before the concert to R.S.V.P.

With that out of the way, my thoughts turned to the still absent Program. Now standing and with a developing sense of concern I asked Kevin if he knew where the Program was. He looked over my right shoulder and said, "It's right behind you Ron." I swung around. Standing right behind me, program in hand, was Mr. Roger Daltrey. We shook hands. His handsome smile told the whole story. "Where did you get this," he asked. Knowing we didn't have time for the long version, I said, "It was a gift from my parents; have either of you ever seen it before?" "No, never." "Thanks for signing and have a really great show," I concluded knowing he was running late. "I'll see you in Phoenix," I added as Roger disappeared out the office door. My heart was pumping. As Kevin finished up some last minute details on his computer he suggested that I stay put for a bit. After slipping out the office door for a moment he returned and told me that they were getting ready to go on. "Come on Ron, we'll join them."

As we exited the office door, I was stunned by what I saw. Lining the intersection of both hallways and for as far as the eye could see were maybe a hundred people: road crew, assistance, security personnel, musicians and at the front of the bisecting lines, Pete Townshend and Roger Daltrey. The stadium crowd was getting anxious as the clapping turned into thunderous rhythmic stomping which seemed to amplify and resonate along the backstage hallways. Suddenly and without warning, Pete put down his guitar and walked away from the line up. I watched the dynamics play out as the word spread in seconds up and down the lines via walky talky and headset intercoms. As abruptly as the concern rose, smiles broke out on everyones faces. The whole tour was on hold. "What's going on?" I asked Kevin. He gave me one of those sheepish smiles and reassuringly stated, "Pete had to take a Pee!"

Two minutes later and with Pete comfortably back in line, we were ready to go. The stadium was physically vibrating with anticipation as the announcement came over the P.A. "Ladies and gentlemen, please welcome The Who." As I walked with Kevin and the band's entourage toward the stage left stairway following close behind drummer Zak Starkey and bassist Simon Townshend and of course Pete and Roger, I was once again reminded just how far one simple act of kindness can go.

I thanked Kevin, The Who's amazingly generous manager, and headed back out to join Linda for the show. In the end, the concert actually brought Linda to tears. She told me later that it was as if they (Roger & Pete) had seen their place in history alongside the other great legends of Woodstock before going out on stage. The performance that night was inspired, the artistry overwhelming as The Who laid themselves flat out for their audience. Had we played a small part or was it just personal emotion we were experiencing? Fact was, it really didn't matter. After all, isn't that what art, well presented, is supposed to do?

the longest winter

More than a dozen years after Johnny Winter had my pen ripped out of his hand in the golf cart by his then manager Teddy Slatus, he was now experiencing a renewed sense of spirit and friendship in his professional relationship with guitarist and promoter Paul Nelson and Company.

My longest Winter began back in 1973 when Linda and I, as teachers at Cloonan Middle School, were living on the bucolic estate of Doris and Al Kaskel, Doral Farms. You will recall that we were living in the gardener's cottage while Frank and Terry Simms rented the converted Herdsman's house right behind (see; The Real Doral Country Club). The following autumn, Steve Paul of The Scene nightclub fame and owner of Blue Sky Records rented the main estate house on OUR island oasis to host what Bebe Buell would later describe as the "Party of the Year," with anyone who was anyone in the east coast Rock and Roll world, in attendance. Our back door neighbor Frank and brother George had by '73 formed their own band, The Simms Brothers Band which won the coveted Battle of the Bands award and title of Connecticut's most popular contemporary group, logistically earning them and us an unofficial invitation to "crash" Paul's soon to be infamous, country picnic/Rock and Roll Extravaganza. Excuse me but this was OUR place remember! You want to party here and have a few friends up for the weekend, we'll be inviting ourselves over for the festivities. And what a night it was. While Linda and I joined Todd Rundgren and blonde beauty Bebe Buell in the master bedroom upstairs, our rising star neighbor Frank Simms hung out in the estate house kitchen and jammed most of the night with Johnny Winter and members of the Edgar Winter group (Edgar was busy shooting pool in the den). Among the invited guests were Bill Graham, owner of the Fillmore East and West Clubs; the entire Edgar Winter Group whose album release of the same year They Only Come Out at Night, featuring the groundbreaking synthesized rock epic, Frankenstein, were circulating about the main estate house. Writers for Rolling Stone, the author Fran Lebowitz, the publicist Carol Strauss, and reportedly scores of other lesser known rising stars like Madonna Ciccone (on whose second album, Like a Virgin, Frank and George would do backup vocals); and Cindy Lauper, who also had Whiter Shade of Pale played at her wedding, joined the revelry.

Paul spared no expense at making the party a smashing success. As reported in both Rolling Stone and later in Rock Scene magazines, "the lavish repast included lemon/lime chicken entrees, sumptuous apricot macaroon mousse and wine served in blue foil-lined wicker picnic baskets, but the real "dirt" about the Doral Bash never made it into print until now.

The Doral Estate mansion was a soft yellow two story center stairway sweeping

Dutch colonial with a circular drive portico entry at the front, set among old growth ever-greens, azaleas and boxwoods. On its south side, the rear of the estate backed up against a near perfectly oval one-acre pond that was a favorite hangout for Canada Geese and the occasional Blue Heron. Two stately cast lanterns and stone pillars held the wrought iron main gates at the bend of the Roxbury Road where the drive crested a gradual hill then descended down the nearly one quarter- mile drive to the estate on the left.

With fellow art prodigy Warren Kahn in tow, we made our way over to the main house at about 7pm, where several hundred guests had already received their welcome baskets with wine and had wasted no time spreading out to every corner of the mansion's proximity. We accepted our dinner basket from catering and en-tered the front door lobby for the first time. The decor was exquisite. Solid walnut wall panels and floors gave way to a billiard room on the left circumscribed by the library and living room and across from the bow-windowed kitchen and first floor family room. Over the course of the next two hours I would find myself sitting on the sofa with Bill Graham while watching Edgar shoot pool with any and all challengers, sharing a doobie with Todd Rundgren and friends, blowing some chick's mind with my Flagship Freedom Stars & Stripes, red, white and blue socks, and hanging out with Frank and Johnny who were jamming most of the night off the kitchen pantry.

Only weeks after the grand gathering of the rock titans and what Linda and I sensed was the end of paradise for the water fowl, red fox and lowly cottage dwell-ers of Doris and Al's sixty acre estate the headline in the Stamford Advocate news-paper read something like, "Body discovered in gang-land style fire and murder that destroys Doral Farm Estate House."

So what, for us, started with a party, fire and gangland style murder in '73, continued at Stratton Mountain, Vermont with an over-protective, embezzling, alco-holic manager in 1993, ended up on a very high note toward the close of 2006, in of all places, New Market, New Hampshire.

We arrived at the Stone Church night spot by mid-afternoon and found that we had preceded everyone except the cook who was prepping for the evening's menu, but who took the time to invite us in to share our Project story and taste a few appetizers. This was like backstage passes with catering,, but our Iron Chef moment was soon broken by the sound of a diesel engine straining to navigate the narrow entry to the adjacent parking lot. Johnny Winters' tour bus had arrived and taken up its position nearest the back door. I spoke to the first person to emerge who turned out to be Johnny's new manager, Paul Nelson. My first impression was of a gentleman who cared deeply for and about the artist he represented and who immediately understood the significance of the Woodstock Project. His suggestion was to wait until the band had a chance to get set up and do the sound check, then he would see about getting together before the show with Johnny.

Lin and I hung out at the bar inside the auditorium while the guys set up and soon found that we were not alone. Paul's wife, had made the trip up for the concert as well and by the time the sound check was over, we had all exchanged web-sites and e-mail addresses. Turns out, the Nelsons, too, lived in Stamford not far from our auspicious Johnny Winter beginning at Doral Farm. Small world.

We had covered every topic from pet adoption to who knew how to get hold of Joshua White, the famous New York liquid light engineer who did the stage lighting backdrop for Woodstock, when Paul came back from the tour bus and said, "Johnny has invited you both to come into his tour bus to do the Program Project." We packed up our gear and followed him outside. Our 30-year wait was about to end. After all the years since his legendary set at Yasgur's Farm, Johnny had seen several copies of the Program but could not verify whether they were the real deal.

We talked about Doral and Woodstock and Slatus and Stratton and how happy he was now. He struck his signature on the page that he shares with Joe Cocker and spoke to The Winter Brothers southern roots;

It's no LIFE rap on picayune non-picker bits, but Crisco stench fried Texas blues and black 3 a.m. misery pangs hell manure bruisesoul, Mr. Winter and his locust screech panhandle unsplendorstrings.

My longest winter ended in winter with the great Mr. Winter, now in the warmest of company and making beautiful music again.

Author's note: Don't forget to download "Meantown Blues" and if he comes to a venue nearby, go. Oh, and tell Johnny, Paul and the gang we say hi.

Top to bottom: The Doral Farm estate house swimming pool.

"Rita" grazing along the quarter mile service entrance fence welcomes us home from school.

The elegant main estate house of Doris and Al Kaskel, circa 1971.

see me, feel me

Sixty days beyond one of the greatest highs of my life, Linda and I would be granted celebrity status by the incomparable Roger Daltrey and Pete Townshend. I kept road manager Kevin's contact information safely stowed away in my wallet as the day grew near. We were staying at the Drake's Casita just a few miles from downtown Phoenix and decided to pay the venue a visit in advance of the concert date.

The U.S. Airways Center's professional liaison turned out to be quite the Rock and Roll junkie himself and we were on the same page right from the start. He showed us around the backstage area, gave us a feel for the layout and talked about his own anticipation of The Who's arrival. After a quick

snack next door and an exchange of cell phone numbers, we were off to call in our R.S.V.P.

Now I know why Kevin gave us three different numbers to call. For days I was unable to get through on any line, then about five days before the concert, perseverance paid off. Kevin had made special arrangements beyond our wildest expectations. The night would start with special guest parking directly outside the staging area and adjacent to the tour buses. "When you get inside to the backstage security checkpoint, ask for me and I'll bring you in for the rest of the night's activities. I think you guys will have a good time."

Kevin's assessment turned out to be the understatement of the century. As we entered the parking garage of the concert venue late in the afternoon of the 28th, the parking attendants moved temporary barriers aside again and again until we found ourselves and our little copper - colored Honda Fit surrounded by Corvettes, Bentleys, Ferraris, Cadillacs and BMWs. But, hey, our brand new little 38 mile per gallon 2007 FIT was the first "new" car we had purchased since leaving teaching in 1978 and one in the first shipment sold in the U.S. so, no Napoleon complex here; we were VIP's. The security window was right inside the stage door. One quick call on the intercom and in short order Kevin met us there and gave us the itinerary for the night. "So, here's what we have planned for you guys. Are you hungry enough to eat?" he inquired. Rule #1, never decline an invitation to eat when you're a guest of, like THE WHO! "We can eat something," we casually responded. "OK great. Pete and Roger have arranged a catered dinner for their guests. It's just getting started so lets walk over to the dining room and I'll get you settled in and check back in about 45 minutes."

I was wearing my Woodstock Program Project T-shirt and jeans, Linda was dressed in a beautiful southwestern style jacket and matching pleated skirt set in Cherokee red with boots to match as we crossed the double doors and into a small intimate, veritable who's who of the entertainment world. Of course the other 75 or so guests are looking at you the same way, with the same interest and curiosity, thinking who's the drop dead gorgeous blonde and what's she doing with that dweeb? Or maybe thinking, what the hell is the Woodstock Program Project? I was sure it was the latter. At first glance and without gawking it seemed that everyone around me looked familiar. Ok, so there's Randy Johnson, pitcher for the Phoenix Suns, and there is no mistaking Alice Cooper who lives in nearby Paradise Valley, but that was as far as I was willing to gawk before sitting down for what turned out to be a three course buffet of steak, seafood, amazing salads and the proverbial fresh fruit compote, the official backstage snack.

Before the hour was up, we got a visit from the center's liaison who approached us to make an introduction. "Ron and Linda, I'd like to introduce you to Alice Cooper." What a nice guy. He had seen my T-shirt and asked to see the Woodstock Program for himself. After paging through for a few minutes we suggested that we all pose for a photo op with the intent of sending out copies to all. Kevin reappeared during the Alice Cooper experience to inform us that Roger was having a tooth ache problem and that they had sent someone out to get Ambisol to kill the pain for the concert. Until then, he was not able to participate in the scheduled meet and greet with his dinner guests. Boy, was I thankful that we had that moment back in Connecticut. But the good news was that we were getting ready to go down the hall to meet up with the legend himself, Jumpin' Pete.

If there is one personality trait that best describes our experience, one on one, with Mr. Townshend it has to be, shy. Pete is a larger than life presence in the room. He's 6' 3" and it could only be observed that his quiet, reserved and commandingly shy persona sort of levels the playing field. It helps place him within the realm of a real approachable easy-to-be-with gentleman. He displayed poise and humble generosity to the degree that I couldn't help but take a chance at posing what could have been misinterpreted as a confrontation, when the first words out of my mouth were, "Pete, I have a bone to pick with you! You made my wife cry at the concert you gave in Connecticut." Pete did not react. In that instant, I knew that a swift clarification was in order. I added, "She was so moved by your performance, it brought her to tears. Thank you for having us as your guests." Pete thanked us in return, signed a few personal items and moved on.

Less than one half hour later, at precisely the moment that the stadium announcer was introducing The Who, Kevin walked us out onto the venue floor and placed us squarely in front of Simon, Zak, Roger and Jumpin' Pete, front row center. Not even a shattered tambourine and tooth ache could diminish the art form of Rock's Royalty that night.

See me, feel me, touch me, heal me. Been there. I can cross that off my bucket list.

Top: After dinner at The Who concert with Alice Cooper and The U.S. Airways Arena staff.

Front row stage right for the final bows — Roger Daltrey and Pete Townshend — The Who, February 28, 2007

Sly and The Family Stone founding members Cynthia Robinson, Jerry Martini and Sister Rose Stone in their dressing room after the show, June 19, 2007.

everyday people

By 2007, younger brother Ken had begun to understand the significance of the Program Project and he gets the credit for letting us know that the Family Stone would be performing at the lucrative Foxwoods Casino in Connecticut. The free concert was held on their nightclub stage within the shopping complex and casino retail wing. Talk about intimate. The club held maybe a couple of hundred patrons and we had secured seats only two rows from the stage.

This show lacked nothing. The three original members Jerry Martini, Cynthia Robinson and "Sister" Rose Stone had collaborated with a younger Sly Stone impersonator to create a strong and harmonic act that brought the audience to their feet as they had almost 40 years earlier at Woodstock.

The group formed back in '67 when Sly and the Stoners combined forces with brother Freddie and the Stone Souls, to bring Jerry, Cynthia, Gregg Errico and Sly together for the first time. Sly and Freddie's sister Rose would join within the year to complete the lineup for the February 1968 Clive Davis release of "Dance to the Music," the group's first national hit. Later the same year the group released their first number one hit single Everyday People, one of the hallmark songs in the Sly & The Family Stone repertoire. The May, 1969 album "Stand" helped secure the band's invitation to play at Yasgur's Farm just three months later, where late in the wee hours of August 17th they gave what has come to be recognized as one of the best performances of the concert.

Immediately after their club show, Cynthia and Rose made an exit for the dressing rooms while Jerry came out to sign autographs and sell CDs. Linda and I waited to be last and we were glad we did. When Jerry saw the Original Woodstock Program for the first time he was visibly moved. "Where are the girls?" he asked one of his assistants. "They went down to change," was the response. "Come with me," Jerry suggested. "This is too important for them to miss," he added as we waited for the elevator to take us down. Moments later we were accompanying founding member Jerry Martini into the dressing room and shaking hands with two beautiful women, trumpeter Cynthia Robinson and keyboardist and singer sister Rose Stone. The rest of the tour gathered around as the three original members signed their page and accepted our "thank you" T-shirts. We did a lot of joking around as we sat at the coffee table in the dressing room but the prize for the best quip of the evening goes to Linda when, after being told by Rose that "This is what we do, you know. We're no different than anybody else, Linda cut her short with, " You mean, you're Everyday People!" I guess some things never get old. Rose broke up and her smile said it all. "You go girl," she shot back. "Yeah we're everyday people." I didn't even try to top that. We walked out in the hall, gave each other big hugs and went on our way vowing to do it again with Sly. I hope, but let's see.

SLY AND THE FAMILY STONE

standing . . . screaming . . . dancing . . . writhing peace
playing music they feel
feeling the music they play; so lend
a mind brother and
dig it!

Sly & The Family Stone's program page. The act's performance was among the most celebrated presentations at Yasgur's Farm. The group went on stage at 3:30 am Sunday morning between Janis Joplin and The Who.

COUNTRY JOE
& THE FISH

all together,
cause we don't give a damn
about old Martha Lorraine
flying high up side of vietnam
with the crystal blues.

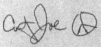

The " Swiffer" guys. Country Joe and I pose for a picture at WBCR radio in Great Barrington, Massachusetts.

country joe

How many of you have made it a Thanksgiving ritual to listen to Alice's Restaurant either just before or after the big meal? Lin and I were able to get an original LP in near mint condition a few years ago and now we just wait for the holiday to come around on the guitar, I mean calendar, and back we go to the years of hope, the years of enlightenment, the years of our discontent, the inspired 60s.

Alice and Ray Brock acquired a deconsecrated church at 4 Van Deusenville Rd. outside of Great Barrington, Massachusetts for $2,000 in 1964. It was here, rather than at Alice's restaurant in a church alley in downtown Stockbridge, that the Thanksgiving dinner that inspired the song took place in '65.

The Guthrie Foundation purchased the church in 1991 and has used it over the years to promote inter-faith cooperation and to stage concerts for dedicated Arlo-phytes.

Our friend Amy had joined the membership of the Guthrie Center and after visiting the famous site ourselves in spring, we did the same; we were now on the official mailing list. July brought news that Country Joe McDonald would be doing a concert there in August. I contacted George, the Director of the Center whom we had met during our visit, and he gave me information I never would have been able to acquire anyplace else. He arranged with a disk jockey at WBCR radio to get us in at the same time Joe was scheduled to be on air for an interview and concert promo.

When we arrived at the Great Barrington station, Joe was already in the studio and on air with DJ-Jeanne Bassis. We waited outside the sound room in the station's reception lobby and listened to a live feed of the conversation inside when asked Joe McDonald what he had been doing lately. "Well I have a great little garden at my house in San Francisco." Elaborating further he went on to describe it as not really organic but a great salad source nonetheless. Pressed again by Jeanne he spilled the beans on another of his OCD activities. "I love to swiffer! Do you know what swiffering is?" he asked. I had my opening line and I used it when she and Joe finally emerged from the sound room. "No way," I said. "You love to swiffer too?" That broke the ice and the rest of the Woodstock Project was one satirical comment after the next, culminating in the ritual passing of the T-shirt and well wishes.

> "All together, cause we don't give a damn
> About old Martha Lorraine
> Flying high up side of Vietnam
> With the crystal blues."
> —Country Joe and the Fish,

Hey Joe, thanks a lot. Now I think of you every time I Swiffer.

Author's note: A few weeks later, DJ Jeanne Basis and WBCR radio invited us back to do a one hour live broadcast dedicated to the Woodstock projects backstories. Jeanne's mid-day show is called "In the Spirit of Play" on WBCR-FM, 97.7 Great Barrington, Mass.

The Guthrie Center, formerly Alice's Restaurant and home of the infamous Thanksgiving dinner and garbage massacree incident, Great Barrington, Massachusetts.

joe cocker
PART ONE

If the date rings a bell, it was only four days after 9/11 that The Guess Who's "American Woman" tour came to the Oakdale Theater, minutes north of Linda's childhood home. The tour was traveling by motor coach and tractor trailer so, as they say in entertainment, the show must go on and America needed the distraction. But we weren't interested in The Guess Who. We had our sights set on the opening act, one Mr. Joe Cocker.

We stopped by the venue early in the afternoon of the concert and approached management there as we had so many times before, elsewhere. Oakdale was unresponsive and uninterested in assisting. No effort would be made here to bring the artist and the historic document together. I couldn't help but think, we had both grown up attending so many events at Oakdale, we didn't deserve being treated with such lack of concern. But then, we hadn't visited the former site of Woodstock, now known as Bethel Woods Center for the Arts, yet.

Ken Evans Photo

Oakdale Theater in Wallingford, Connecticut was the site of my first attempt at getting together with the English Gentleman, Mr. Joe Cocker.

joe cocker
PART TWO

It had been almost 20 years since Linda and I had last visited The Garden. You'll remember that on that auspicious occasion, Alan Gerry had just purchased Yasgur's Farm along with another 1,000 acres surrounding the Woodstock site and had begun re-branding nature's beauty into "Gerry-land".

On the 4th of July 2008, I found out that Joe Cocker would be appearing at Bethel Woods, opening for The Steve Miller Band the following weekend on July 13th. We decided to get to the venue after lunch to give ourselves plenty of time to make arrangements prior to show time.

We arrived before sound check and before the grounds

were officially opened for the night's activities and went directly to the reception desk where we were greeted by Sarah who introduced us to Jenise, Tara and Amber, all receptionists in the box office. . After Sarah contacted the manager's office she took the time to introduce us to Wade Lawrence who was the director of The Museum dedicated to the legacy of Woodstock. We showed him the Project and he was genuinely enthralled, but not enough to offer us for a quick walk through the Museum before working out evening arrangements with Bethel Woods management. Sarah suggested that we have a seat in the lobby. The venue liaison Suzanne Rapone would be out shortly to help us.. One hour later we were still waiting. When the waiting game got too uncomfortable, we broke the monotony with a walk about the grounds after being given strict details about where we could and could not go. The grounds of the site were immaculately landscaped, irrigated and fertilized to perfection with not a blade of grass out of place. Ascending and descending walkways cut through flowerbeds of new growth perennials and brilliantly colored annuals beyond the outdoor café. It was like visiting a Hilton, but with checkpoints and hippie look alikes vending coffee and baked goods from a "Twelve Tribes" concession stand located at the crest of the hill that you might know from the cover of the Woodstock Album. Upon our return to the visitor's center, still no news. After yet another hour of waiting, I guess the venue manager felt we were serious enough to merit a moment of her time.

We ran through the routine again for Suzanne but she was adamant that the best she could do was take it down to the theater herself and get it signed. You know what answer that provoked. Still, we did our best to keep a jovial and upbeat attitude as the afternoon wore on. We were kept under surveillance, while the venue manager supposedly made every effort on our behalf to "see what she could do" to arrange access. I guess they were expecting us to behave in a defiant manner. That's just not who we are. The unimaginable turn of events that followed left Linda and me physically weakened and emotionally abused.

Bethel Woods management had now jerked us around for more than six hours and the concert auditorium was near capacity, with Joe Cocker getting ready to open the show when we got word from Suzanne that we should meet her at the backstage gate. When asked how to get to that gate, she told us to proceed along the Theater Walk and take a right at the first Water Feature. "The What?" I asked. "The Water Feature," she reiterated. "What's a Water Feature?" I was honestly stumped on this one. "You know, it's like a fountain and sculpture pond." Linda and I looked at each other and rolled our eyes. The Grande Illusion had finally hit home. Woodstock had been reconstituted into the antithesis of itself by the very people who never got it, right from the start.

We approached the gate and gave security there our names and management instructions. They gave us the green light and told us we could find her through the main backstage doors under the awning. We proceeded to the outside veranda where we got into a conversation with some of the tour people who were interested in the Woodstock Project themselves, when suddenly Suzanne came charging out of the backstage doors and began screaming at us. "What the hell are you doing here?" she insisted. "You told us to meet you here," I responded. "You can't be here. You have to leave immediately or I will have to call security," she demanded as she accompanied us down the stairs and out to the security gate, stage left. "Stay here until I get back to you," were our orders. By now it had begun to rain steadily and heavily and the air temperature had dropped to perhaps the upper 50s or low 60s. And there we stood in the windswept rain for the duration of the evening's presentation, our security guard insisting that she kept reminding Suzanne that we were still waiting in the freezing rain. Suzanne never bothered making contact with us again.

"It was a dark and dreary night" and we were both drenched and chilled to the bone by the time we left the post that we had been told to stay at. The concert audience had left and there we stood abandoned by Bethel Woods management after doing everything they had asked us to do. We were in shock. No artist, venue or management had ever abused us in a way that could endanger our health & well-being before. But the real kicker came as we made our way past one of the exit security checkpoints and struck up a conversation with the guard there. After telling him what kind of treatment we had just been subjected to by the management, he proceeded to spill the beans about the methods and procedures employed by Alan Gerry and the Bethel Woods Art Center operation. "I have worked for the New York State Prison system, I have worked for Federal government and I have worked for some of the nation's largest private security firms, and in all my years I have never seen anything even remotely close to the surveillance and security that I have seen here," he concurred. "This place is on lockdown 24/7." It didn't surprise our security guard one bit when we told him what just happened. I wasn't going to let this one go without contacting the people at the top.

Back home at my computer, a quick web search brought me to the offices for Bethel Woods located in Alan Gerry's hometown of Liberty. I called and made contact with Gerry's secretary, Darlene Fedun, who was somewhat skeptical about the whole affair but willing to hear me out. I told her that I would be chronicling the entire incident and sending a letter to Mr. Gerry. In subsequent phone conversations and after receipt of my letter, Ms. Fedun said she would "Look into it" while not offering any mediation or response to our mistreatment. In the end, Gerry chose to drop the whole incident; refusing to respond to my letter at all. What would you have done? Yes, Lin and I vowed to never go back to what was once THE symbol for a generation of an open and free society. Mr.Gerry et.al: morally, ethically and philosophically, you have made a mockery of Woodstock, and all your money can't hide the truth. Starting today, America demands restitution. How could your staff treat anyone with such disregard and disrespect? They say it always starts at the top!

Ms. Suzanne Rapone

Venue Liaison / Bethel Woods

PO Box 222

Liberty. N.Y. 12754

July 14, 2008

Re; Joe Cocker

Dear Suzanne;

Linda and I have just returned from our 500 mile round trip to Bethel Woods where, as you now know, our Woodstock Program Project failed and I wish to follow up herein.

This 25 year project has always been about honoring not only the artists that made the 1969 event historic but my now 90 year old parents whose simple act of kindness on August 18th of that year epitomizes the essence of the Woodstock experience and to whom this project is dedicated.

We have tried to piece together the sequence of events of yesterday and at what point everything changed from seemed to be a friendly and cooperative mutual effort between us.

We had arrived early to your venue as we always try to do and after meeting and speaking with Sarah, Jenise, Tara, Amber and of course Wade Lawrence at the visitors center and after giving them all a taste of the project and a copy of the advance promotional and history, you were contacted to assist in our effort.

Joe Cocker is one of only a handful of artists who remain as non-participants in this historic effort.

We respected your early offer to take this document down to the venue and get it signed for us, but, as we explained, it has only been out of our sight once in the 39 years and as it turned out, Carlos Santana's brother Jorge was enjoying it in his dressing room when we arrived there. Because of its rare singular status, we vowed to never let that happen again.

Returning, you told us that you had arranged to get us as far as the backstage "checkpoint" if we would trust you to take it in, get it signed and bring it right back; we agreed. Bill Berthauf (sp) was asked to help bring us down when the time was right and this is where we think the communications broke down. It had now been 4 hours since our arrival at Bethel Woods and we needed a break, so we drove down to the monument. By the time we returned, we didn't know if we had missed your call to Bill, so we approached Bonnie with security and asked her if Bill had been looking for us? Bonnie instead called Bill and told him that Ron and Linda were ready to be picked up. I immediately told her that I just wanted to know if Suzanne had tried to reach us.? Bill arrived minutes later and said, "Let's go, Suzanne will meet you when she is ready." He brought us outside backstage where we met Bob Adams and Dawn when suddenly we were told we had to leave immediately; as if we had done something terribly wrong.

From that moment on, everything changed. We were left out in the pouring rain for hours with a promise from you personally that you would come and get us, while every effort to communicate with you was ignored. Bill suddenly didn't care about us anymore while Press and guest passes were being given out to many others and those I've worked with over the years such as Elliott Landy and Linda shared the backstage activities just yards away.

Not since the Grateful Dead ten years ago Suzanne have we been treated with such disrespect and arrogant indifference by a venue.

We did everything we were asked to do over the nine hours we patiently waited to have just 1 minute with Joe Cocker, take a picture, give him our T-shirt, sign the program and make a little history. Instead, in the end we were blown off, forgotten and left out in the rain by non-other than the actual site that is supposed to symbolize sharing, caring and love; the place where it all began 39 years ago.

We will chronicle our experience for future generations as our project nears its end. The irony is that Wade had hinted to us that he knew of a museum that would love to have such a unique project.

I may never return now to what was once "The Garden" Suzanne and perhaps the Smithsonian will show us a modicum of respect.

That can be your legacy!

Ron and Linda Evans

A copy of the Suzanne Rapone letter was sent to Allan Gerry's personal secretary, Darlene Fedun. She said she would look into the circumstances surrounding July 13th . Weeks later I received a phone call. I was told by Darlene that they were still looking into the situation and that they would "make it up to us if we ever decided to try Bethel Woods again".

I believe in giving people the benefit of the doubt. The following summer, (2009) marked the 40th anniversary of Woodstock and something BIG would surely be planned for the occasion. By late April, word began circulating that a national tour was being planned and that Bethel Woods of course got first dibs on August 15th. On May 16, 2009 , I drafted the following letter to Allan Gerry and Darlene Fedun:

Alan Gerry & Darlene   May 16, 2009
PO Box 222
Liberty, N.Y. 12754

Dear Darlene;

So it is the 40th anniversary of Woodstock and after the way we were treated last year at the Joe Cocker event, we vowed never to go back … then you called and offered to make it up to us if we ever decided to try again. Here is my try.

I understand that you are hosting the "Legends of Woodstock" concert on the 15th of August. Among your guests are original members of Canned Heat and Big Brother, neither of whom have signed or been given T-shirts of the project. Would Bethel Woods be interested in assisting or perhaps sponsoring (non-financially) our presence at this event? Providing access and making us feel welcome would be all that is needed.

Our project is planned to proceed until the 50th.

If you wish to contact us, my cell is 802 *** ****.

Cordially,

Ron Evans

Here is the final correspondence I sent to Alan Gerry and Darlene Fedun, the CEO and his assistant at Bethel Woods Performing Arts Center days after the Heroes of Woodstock 40th Anniversary Concert Tour.

Alan Gerry & Darlene Fedun   August 19, 2009

PO Box 222

Liberty, N.Y. 12754

Congratulations!

This past Saturday, the well funded illusionist team of Gerry & Fedun seems to have pulled off another well rehearsed deception in the garden … for only $19.69. Such a deal; an all star line-up, a 40th anniversary and a wedding (Leslie West of Mountain got married on stage that weekend) for about the same price as dinner at McDonalds. I'm thinking that I could have pulled in 17,000 to my house had I made the same briberous offer.

Darlene, after last years abuse at the hands of Suzanne Rapone, I'm so glad I made the decision back in May to give Bethel Woods an opportunity to make it up to us as you offered to do. At least now the record is clear.

You'll recall that after receiving my letter of 5/26/09 requesting your help in doing the Program Project at your venue on the 40th anniversary, you replied that you would see what you could do … "Send me the info". I did.

Weeks, then months went by until, with only 10 days left before the event, I get the Grandest Illusion of them all; that you've been sending requests to the bands, but no one has answered!

Does the name Tim Murphy ring a bell? How about GenX? In less than 4 hours, using only my cell phone with e-mail, I had two guest passes waiting for me at Foxwoods the night before your event. We spent almost the entire evening backstage and in the dressing rooms with ALL the Heroes of Woodstock as guests of both the venue and Sam Andrews & Co. It was a memorable and historic evening for the artists as well as for the Original Woodstock Program Project.

So, thanks for proving to Linda and me what you are made of, yet again. I hear that your Blackwater Security Force was nowhere to be seen on August 15th. Checkpoints "Alpha" and "Bravo" made sure they weren't necessary. Wouldn't want anything resembling Woodstock to spoil the illusion.

On the day of your pathetic deception, Linda and I went up to Woodstock, N.Y. where, in an intimate café, Gilles Malkine, a guitarist who played with Tim Hardin on Yasgur's Farm back in '69, was signing the Program and celebrating the historic weekend with about 100 of his closest friends. As we drove away, the towns fireworks display began and Gilles was preparing to jump start his career with 3 encores and 3 standing ovations … and therein lies the soul of Woodstock, a place it's doubtful you'll ever find.

Ron Evans

Joe belts out, with a little help from his friends, at the South Shore Music Circus in Cohassett, Massachusetts, July 2, 2009.

After show in the hospitality room with a true british gentleman!

joe cocker
PART THREE

Third time is the charm? After blatant disregard at Oakdale Theater in Connecticut followed by physical and psychological abuse at the hands of Bethel Woods Center for the Arts management, I decided to going straight to the artist.

By 2009 the internet had come to wireless and for the first time Lin and I were able to do some personal research on her cell phone. Turns out that Joe Cocker and his wife Pam purchased a substantial piece of property in the remote western town of Crawford, Colorado where they created the Cocker Kids Foundation, a non-profit dedicated to helping children achieve personal goals through responsibility and accountability. Mad Dog Ranch, built between 1993 and 1995 includes the Cockers' splendid 17,000 sq. ft. English Tudor home. A single phone call to Cathy Schelle, the foundation's administrator, put me in touch with Joe's wife Pam, who in turn helped arrange a meet-up with the Woodstock legend himself during his solo tour at the most intimate of venues, The South Shore Music Circus in Cohasset, Massachusetts, on July 2nd of the same year as the 40th anniversary of Woodstock.

Joe's road manager Ray was right on top of it. He e-mailed his contact info to me and I wasted no time in getting him the promo packet for the Project, the good old fashion way, via snail mail. Upon receipt, things moved swiftly and by the end of the month Ray had arranged not only show tickets, compliments of the artist, but after show access to the tour's meeting and dressing room suite. After almost a decade of refusals, our efforts to share the Program with another icon of Woodstock had finally fallen upon friendly and caring ears. Joe's family and staff back home were kind and expeditious. Suzanne at The South Shore Music Circus was awesome, opening her doors to our efforts. Ray made us feel welcome and set us up for an historic evening, but most of all it was the legend himself, the Honorable Mr. Joe Cocker, who ended up completely blowing us away on July 2, 2009.

To appreciate the dynamics of the concert, it must be pointed out that The Music Circus is located south of Boston, in a most magnificent New England coastline village where one gets the feeling of being surrounded by clam boats and cranberry bogs. The theater is in the round and sloped so as to afford every one of the 2,300 attendees a perfectly intimate view not more than 50 feet from the rotating stage below.

Judging from the demographics of the audience, you never would have guessed that the artist about to take the stage was best known for his erratic drug-induced gesticulations and aging hippie persona. Lin and I were stunned. From the moment Joe took the stage until the very last encore we watched the audience, half made up of teenage girls, enthusiastically singing the words to every song Joe pulled out of his repertoire, then raising their arms in unison to Joe's every jump. Yes, you read that correctly. Evidently, Jumpin' Pete's not the only aging hippie rocker that brings the house down when he pulls off the old gravity-defying maneuver. Even when an inebriated patron decided to stand up right in back of us and walk down to join Joe Cocker on stage for a little quality alone time with the artist, Joe handled himself with poise and control. Before being escorted back to her seat, she whispered sweet nothings into Joe's ear but the consummate professional didn't miss a beat and the teenage girls crooned even louder.

Two encores later, the artist and the audience alike were at once exhilarated and exhausted. It was an emotional dichotomy; a psychosomatic "extreme sports" kind of catharsis. The artist had given it up and the crowd talk on the way out was inspired. For Linda and me the exhilaration was about to hit hyper-space.

Only four people were granted after show access on this occasion. The others had an album cover that they were looking to get signed so we would wait to go after them. We were brought into a pressroom while Mr. Cocker showered and changed for the after-show. I will tell you, I didn't know what to expect of the artist's demeanor or personality. Would he be easy to communicate with? My background is sports medicine, so I wondered if he would display symptoms of fine motor skill dysfunction?

As we were standing about the conference tables sharing the Woodstock Program with the rest of the band and tour entourage, the banter ceased for just a moment as the Legend entered the room. Dressed in a sport jacket and silk shirt, freshly showered and very distinguished, the dapper Mr. Joe Cocker spoke with a clear and audible English accent, the almost spastic gestures of his stage presentation had vanished. . Our off-stage host was the embodiment of a soft spoken English gent Our moment had, at long last, come. After the album signing, the evening was ours. Joe revealed that he had never seen the Original Woodstock Program and after paging through it with us, asked his tour to gather around for the signing. "This is an historic document. I want you all to be part of this moment," Joe announced. We had lived to see another scribe, the elusive Joe Cocker, put his mark on our Woodstock memento.

Before we said our goodbyes, I assured Joe that I would keep the program in a safe place. I gave him my word. , "Speaking of words, I have to ask you, What did the lady who walked up on stage during your performance say to you?" Gesturing toward my ear, he reiterated, "She said, I know you! And you know me! with a thick German accent". Joe raised his eyebrows and tipped his head in defiance. Just another day in the life of a rock star, getting by with a little help from his friends: on and off stage.

To donate to Joe Cocker's non-profit for kids; info@cockerkidsfoundation.com

Mail; Cocker Kids P.O.Box 404 Crawford, CO 81415

Please mention "Chasing Woodstock"

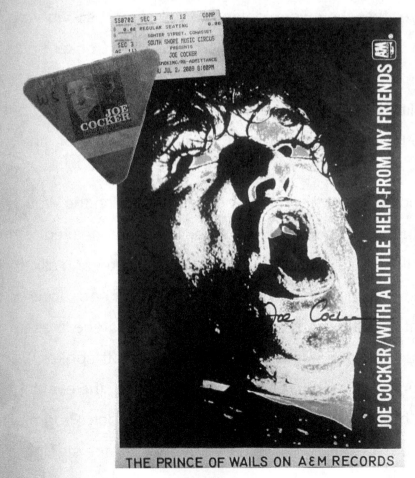

heroes of woodstock
40TH ANNIVERSERY TOUR

The high we reached with Joe Cocker lasted well into the start of our efforts to gain access for what was being billed as the Official Woodstock Anniversary Tour or The Heroes of Woodstock. The compilation consisting of Jefferson Starship, Ten Years After, Canned Heat, Big Brother and the Holding Company, Tom Constanten of the Grateful Dead and Country Joe McDonald was preparing to do a three month national celebration beginning and ending in Mount Pleasant, Michigan, on August 1st and October 10th respectively. I had a decision to make. It seemed only fitting that such an event should be celebrated at the site of the original concert but after the way we had been mistreated, why would we even consider giving them another chance? At this point I suspect you have come to know me well enough to figure out what that decision was.

Everyone deserves another chance. Right after Joe Cocker, I placed a call to Darlene Fedun at Bethel Woods and told her that we wanted to make arrangements to do the Woodstock Project at the original site with the Heroes of Woodstock. Her help would be appreciated. "I'll see what I can do," was her somewhat evasive answer. It was still early July and the tour was scheduled to perform there on August 15th , almost 40 years to the day that Woodstock took place, so we had plenty of time to make this happen. My hope, of course, was that Darlene, Alan Gerry, et.al would take this opportunity to make amends by affording our humble project the experience of a lifetime for the big 40.

Just to be sure, I sent off another Project Promo Packet to Bethel Woods in case the road manager needed verification. Still, after weeks of waiting, no answer from Darlene. With the last two weeks before the concert approaching, I decided to ask for her e-mail in order to expedite the process but as you can see from my letter, Bethel Woods hadn't changed their stripes. I was getting the old "Sorry but we can't seem to contact anyone from the tour" BS. Alan Gerry and Company had over a month to do something dynamic and inspiring at their Yasgur's Farm 40th Anniversary Heroes event but they chose, once again, to deceive and mislead us. Really? How do you host a concert tour at a major venue and not have anyone representing the artists to answer your inquiries? Does this mean that Bethel Woods Center for the Arts has no say in the process? Do they just wait around and hope that the scheduled acts show up? Well I wasn't waiting any longer.

We were at one week and counting when I set out to undo what Gerry had done. A search on line revealed that the Heroes Tour would be making a stop at the MGM/Foxwoods Resort on the 14th, the day before Bethel Woods. I needed a direct contact. Although Big Brother and the Holding Company had not played with Janis

Joplin back in '69, they had been such an integral part of her career that I would be proud to have them participate. It took some work, but eventually I was able to get Sam Andrew's personal e-mail address and when I explained my mission to him, he offered to help. As you can see from the August 6th e-mail to Foxwoods' management, they welcomed us back with open arms and set us up with complimentary tickets for the night. Sam Andrew gave us the green light to meet him after the show and agreed to bring us backstage to do the Project with everyone who wanted to participate. In less than 48 hours we had accomplished what Bethel Woods told us, for more than a month, could not be done.

Foxwoods' liaison Lisa made the extra effort to obtain two additional guest passes for Sam Andrew and to leave them for us at Will Call, making our arrival at Foxwoods easy. Remember, we were told that Sam and his Big Brother co-artists would meet us after the show and I'm a literal kind of guy so, when Big Brother finished their set and Jefferson Starship prepared to take the stage, I was waiting for the entire show to be over before going into action. Some ten minutes into Starship, a light bulb went off in my head. Shit. Something's not kosher.

I had a hunch about that 15 minute rule. Linda stayed at our seats while I went up to the lobby of the auditorium to check things out. I caught a glimpse of some fans standing around an autograph table with two artists signing album covers. They seemed to be just finishing up. I asked if Sam Andrew was around and introduced myself. "He has already gone up to his room," I was told. I knew it. Always trust the 15 minute rule. "If you'll hang here for just a few minutes, I can take you backstage. I'm getting ready to head there myself. I'm Peter Albin and this is David Getz." I ran back to get Linda as Peter worked with security and stage personnel for clearance. After some wrangling, we got the go. "Stay with me," Peter suggested. "Once we're in, you'll be all set." We hugged his heels as security guided us through a maze of hallways and checkpoints finally emerging offstage right in a crowd of family, friends and artists waiting to go on. Country Joe was sitting on a black prop box when I got the sudden urge to see if he would remember me from WBCR radio. "Hey Joe," I knelt down and spun around for him to see the Woodstock Program Project T-shirt I was wearing. "Look familiar," I asked. "Yah, you're the Swiffer Guy!" Really? I thought, for this aging hippie, life couldn't get any better. But I was wrong.

From stage right Peter, Linda, myself and a few roadies hopped into a nearby elevator and zipped up a couple of floors. When the doors opened we were smack dab in the middle the artist's suites and media/meeting rooms.

First stop, the tour's meeting room, which, for this event had been converted into a tearoom for Alice, complete with the Mad Hatter, the Hooka Smoking Caterpillar and the Cheshire Cat. Peter introduced us to Tom Constanten, "The Mad Hatter" who was already up and about hosting the tea party. When Tom found out what we were doing he wanted in. "Did you play at Woodstock?" I naively asked. "I played with The Grateful Dead!" Oh fuck, what do I do now. I had promised myself I would never let anyone from that group of losers go near The Program again. But then, the Mad Hatter, with his jovial and engaging personality practically had me at hello. I was rendered helpless by his warmth and good nature. "You'll be my sole representative from The Dead," I guaranteed him. Tom was cool with that, as he added his signature to the macabre center double truck Dead page of The Program and graciously accepted our commemorative T-shirt for participating. He wasted no time putting it to good use. Ripping off the tee he had on and replaced it with ours was a first. T.C., the Harvard Ph.D, was going on stage in about 15 minutes as a guest keyboardist for Jefferson Starship and he was going to be wearing our shirt. Very Cool Mr. Hatter.

As we fooled around with Tom and the two Woodstock veterans of Starship, Marty Balin (the Hooka Smoking Caterpiller) and Paul Kantner (the Cheshire Cat) passed around a doobie which we graciously declined (Hey, we were working here), our tour host returned to let us know that Canned Heat was in their dressing room and interested as well. I felt like a kid in a candy store, figuratively speaking. Before we were able to walk the two doors down past the elevator lobby we bumped into

Fito de la Parra, Canned Heat drummer and vocalis,who was out in the hallway with Harvey Mandel. Our host left us in their good hands and hastened away to manage the show while Fito and Harvey invited us into their dressing room to check out the Program.

The Foxwoods suites weren't just dressing rooms. They each consisted of an outer common media or greeting room circumscribed by several private inner changing, dressing and make up rooms. We decided to make ourselves comfortable around a bar-like high top with cushioned stool seats and space for about six. By the time the artists' wives and tour members dropped by for a look, we were making the commotion of an impromptu group grope. Suddenly, Harvey heard groaning coming from the dressing room directly behind him. I didn't get it, but fellow artist Harvey Mandel did. He broke away from our little celebration and headed straight back in that direction while the rest of us continued our shenanigans at Table One.

Moments later Gibson/Les Paul afficianado Harvey returned with a third party. The look on both their faces was priceless. Harvey displayed an air of apologetic empathy as he introduced us to his forlorn friend and fellow Canned Heat legend and Fender/Stand up bassist extraordinaire, Mr. Larry Taylor. The expression on Larry's face was classic "unloved puppy." He had been back in his dressing room, heard all the commotion out in the media room and wondered what was going on.

I couldn't help myself. It just came out. "Larry," I pronounced, "this is only for those who played Woodstock." Harvey interceded on Larry's behalf. "He was at Woodstock!" "Are you certain?" I shot back. Sometimes those who were there don't remember they were there. Larry had heard enough and was emboldened to challenge me. "OK never mind, now I don't want to sign," he insisted. "I'm going back to my dress room," but you could see that he was playing me too. It took all six of us ganging up on him to lure him back to the table. Fito, Harvey and his wife, Larry's wife, Linda and me all begging him to come back. When we finally got that little jesting behind us, Larry turned out to be just the sweetest and most personable guy you could ever know. We spent the better part of half and hour while he and his wife talked with us about visual vs. auditory art, The Program Project, remembrances of that historic weekend and being on the road. After exchanging contact information, we thanked them all for their kind generosity and made our way down the elevator to the stage where Jefferson Starship was winding down their set with We Built This City and keyboardist, Tom Constanten, was proudly displaying our Woodstock T-shirt, stage right. Country Joe was still sitting right where I left him about an hour and a half ago. He was the emcee for the Heroes Tour, so I'm sure it was up and down for him the whole evening. But here is the real irony. The guy who made the whole evening happen for us was the one guy we had missed after the show and he turned out to be the only member of Big Brother and the Holding Company who actually played with Janis Joplin and The Kozmic Blues Band at Woodstock. Sam Andrew, if you're reading this, thanks for everything and please lets get together soon. I have a very important question to ask you.

Heroes of Woodstock national tour, August 14, 2009. Foxwoods Resort, Connecticut. Top to bottom:

David Getz signs the Woodstock program.

Peter Albin and David Getz, Big Brother & the Holding Co. pose for Linda after signing.

Fito de la Parra and Harvey Mandell pose with the Woodstock program as Larry Taylor plays hard to get, behind.

Harvey Mandell, Canned Heat, gets an earful of Woodstock project details outside his dressing room at the 40th Heroes Tour, Foxwoods.

The very personable Grateful Dead key-boardist, Tom Constantine takes a break from the tea party.

Harvey looks on as Larry Taylor breaks his boycott.

Gilles Malkine at the Alchemy Cafe, Woodstock,
New York, August 15, 2009.

gilles malkine
TIM HARDIN BAND

My internet search to find an alternative to the Bethel
Woods fiasco had also landed me on a Woodstock, New York
events site and to the discovery that Gilles Malkine was going
to be appearing at a great little café and night spot just north
of the iconic village center. Upon securing our 40th Anniversary Heroes Tour access at Foxwoods, we thought that if Gilles
would consent to doing the Project, we would lay over somewhere in Connecticut or Massachusetts, then drive over to the
town for which the historic concert was named for a more
intimate close to an otherwise whirlwind weekend.

As you can see from the e-mails, Gilles was not an easy

sell. I've been around the business long enough to know that he had good reason to be skeptical. His 1969 Woodstock performance on stage with folk artist and long-time friend Tim Hardin was both bitter and sweet. Harden, who brought a heroin addiction back with him from Vietnam, circa 1959-60, rose to stardom with the writing of "If I were a Carpenter" made famous with Bobby Darin's 1966 album release of the same name. Hardin had contributed four additional tracks to Darin's Top Ten single to help create the chart-winning folk rock metamorphosis album.

Linda and I caught up to Gilles almost 30 years after Tim had finally succumbed to an on again, off again relationship with his heroin habit. We arrived at the Alchemy Café in the early afternoon and immediately got a good feeling about our decision. This very intimate single level Adirondack style restaurant/bar/café set amidst ancient conifers and joined by boutique and artisan shops and a country theater, was the perfect place to be with friends; even those friends you have never met.

We did the Woodstock Program Project before Gilles went on. He had seen several copies which he thought were original play bills but described subtle differences from ours. As he paged through, he came to Tim's page and lingered. Gilles memories came racing back. "I don't know why they felt compelled to show Tim coming out of a Poppy plant," he reminisced. "Tim never held that against them, but I think it was insensitive," Malkine reminisced. I wanted Gilles to know that the choice of where to sign was solely his to make. Ultimately, he chose to share his place in Woodstock history with his longtime friend and musical companion right across from another legendary guitarist, Jeff Beck.

The intimate crowd that came to hear Gilles play this day consisted of all close personal friends and proud followers of their hometown Woodstock veteran. To welcome Linda and me into that circle, he dedicated one of his many satirical classics to us during the show. Sung to the melody of "Big Rock Candy Mountain", Gilles belted out "Big Vermont-ie Mountain". We were instant groupies. The pride on display and the intimate setting could not have been a more fitting environment to close out a most memorable 40th anniversary weekend. Gilles boasted that his Program Project participation had "Revived his lackluster career," as he shyly answered one ovation after another. Our hearts were full of pride and contentment as we said our goodbyes and dusk turned to darkness over the Slide Mountain valley to our west and we headed back Tinker Road toward Woodstock Village.

Suddenly, a flash of light broke through the darkened sky from directly ahead. Moments later, a thunderous boom followed by another brilliant flash. As we cleared the tall pines north of town the source of the distraction came into view. It was Woodstock celebrating "Woodstock", 40 years on. We pulled our little FIT car to the side of the road and had a good tearful hug. As the fireworks exploded overhead, we were reminded how important it is to follow your dreams. If the path you choose is the right one, the reward will be the consequence. Our hearts were with our new friends and Gilles, our unsung hero of Woodstock.

worn corduroy funk strummer, creepingcreeping to the airmobile hangar to free the shadow machines that moan with the seventh sun at the red white and blue moon.

POPPY C. v. d. P.
Papaveraceae Timae Hardinaceae

Gilles chooses to honor his fellow folk artist Tim Hardin
by signing the controversial Poppy page of the program.

Alan's prized first promo pressing of Sha-Na-Na's first album.

alan cooper
SHA-NA-NA

Back on July 2nd when we arrived at the South Shore Music Circus to have our unforgettable evening with Joe Cocker, we had noticed that one of the other acts scheduled to play there that summer was Bowser's Doo-Wop Review starring the charismatic lead singer and cut up for Sha-Na-Na, John (Bauman) Bowser. I asked Suzanne, our liaison there, if she would get into touch with John for the Program. She got back with the information that Bowser did not play Woodstock in 1969. "Evidently he replaced another founding member of the group named Alan Cooper," she relayed. I went to work on Linda's smart phone (technology has come a long way since Univac) and to my surprise Alan Cooper was alive and well and living a stone's throw from our friends in Orange, New Jersey.

After making history on the Woodstock stage just before Jimi Hendrix's finale the morning of Monday, August 18th, 1969, Alan finished up his undergraduate studies at Columbia, took some time off to travel, then returned to complete his MA of Philosophy and Ph.D.in Religious Studies at Yale. I chased Alan down at the Jewish Theological Seminary in Manhattan where, several e-mails and one posted delivery later, we earned his trust and he consented to give a look at the Program Project. We were going to be traveling right past his home town on the way south for the winter and when he and his wife, Tamar, offered to host us at their home, we were ecstatic.

The Coopers live in an elegant Dutch Colonial Revival style brick home in the quaint gas-lit village of South Orange. We felt at home the moment we stepped into the bright, somewhat eclectic, richly academic living room, sat down on comfy leather couches and spent the next two hours cavorting like long lost family.

Alan began by giving us some background on the evolution of Sha-Na-Na. He credited group member Rob Leonard's brother George for coming up with not only the group's name, but with the idea of using costumes to emphasize their stage personas and with developing the choreographic satire that, by 1968, became the groups M.O. After the riots of the same year, Columbia University was itching to promote non-political concert events and Sha-Na-Na was born.

Alan explained how he and Joe Witkin, the group's keyboard player, went out cruising New York City for gigs and ended up at The Scene, where owner Steve Paul was busy promoting Johnny Winter as the "next Beatles." "When Bert Sommer brought his friend Michael Lang into the club to hear the boys from Columbia, Lang wanted them for his upcountry festival, but when Jimi Hendrix fell in to love with Sha-Na-Na's antics, the negotiations began. Jimi's unwavering demands were simple; #1 "I want to close out the concert" and #2 "I want to play with those guys!"

Alan explains. As history recounts, the negotiations could not have lasted very long.

Finally, Alan talked to us about driving up to Woodstock and staying with his friend Sam Gladstone who lived close enough to the site that they were able to walk to the concert. He recalled having dinner and sharing champagne back stage with Ric Lee and the Ten Years After band the night before their early morning performance. Both he and Tamar seemed a bit shy and yet nostalgic about revisiting Alan's 15 minutes of entertainment fame. But when he opened the Program and spotted Jocko and Donny's signatures on the amazing sunburst designed first page, a smile came over his face and he thoughtfully signed, "Thanks for the great visit!" Alan Cooper - Sha-Na-Na.

There's one last very cool thing I need to share with you about our afternoon with the Sha-Na-Na vocalist. When I told Alan about my little vinyl album collection back home he shuffled off to the next room and came back with a mint condition, original pressing advance Promotional copy of Sha-Na-Na's very first album, the '69 release "Rock & Roll Is Hear To Stay," and before I even had a chance to ask the question, he looked me straight in the eye and said, "No, it's not for sale!" But, Alan my good friend! If you ever come across another copy in mint condition, I'm still here. And the invitation is open for you and Tamar to hear it on the La Chateau Records monitors at our home in Vermont.

Alan & Tamar Cooper at home in South Orange, New Jersey.

REMEMBER THEN · COME GO WITH ME · BOOK OF LOVE · LITTLE GIRL OF MINE · TEEN ANGEL
LITTLE DARLIN' · SILHOUETTES · HEARTBREAK HOTEL · A TEENAGER IN LOVE · LONG TALL SALLY
CHANTILLY LACE · YOUNG LOVE · LOVERS NEVER SAY GOODBYE · ROCK & ROLL IS HERE TO STAY

A KAMA SUTRA PRODUCTION
PRODUCED AND DIRECTED BY ARTIE RIPP

Top photo: Allan pages through the Woodstock Program in his living room after signing.
Bottom photo: Back cover of Sha-Na-Na's debut album.

After a most memorable interview in the teachers lounge at the University of Dayton Law school, April 6, 2011

michael lang
WOODSTOCK PRODUCER

Over the decades of doing the Woodstock Program Project, I made numerous attempts to contact Michael Lang, the mastermind behind the concert, all to no avail. This year would be the game changer. Lang had added his contribution to the 40th Anniversary celebration with the release of his book, The Road to Woodstock, co-authored by Holly George-Warren, the award winning writer of "Grateful Dead 365"and he was scheduled to make a stop at one of New England's most exciting and comprehensive bookstores. The Northshire Bookstore in Manchester, Vermont was hosting Michael and Holly for a presentation and book signing to be filmed by C-Span for Book TV.

Upstairs in Northshire's presentation room, Michael

gave a lusterless verbal synopsis of the making of the concert and when asked "Can you tell us how many copies of the Program were printed for the original event?" he insisted that the number was 100,000. Still selling the event, Michael? With only a week to go before the concert, Woodstock Promotions had pre-sold about 35,000 tickets. Why then would they pay to print one hundred thousand programs? Unless Michael can show me the invoice from Concert Promotions, I'm sticking with Lee Blumer's account.

After a short break, Michael and Holly regrouped downstairs for the signing. I had the Project and a copy of Road in tow as I made my way to the front of the line. The whole experience with Lang was so very anti-climactic. Sign the Program. Smile for the camera. Take the picture. OK, next! Holly, on the other hand, was warm and engaging, taking the time to express her genuine interest in the whole idea behind the effort. What was the take away for me on this one? Well, at least I know now why he never answered my e-mails!

The cover of my Original Woodstock Program, one of few to survive the deluge and subsequent mud-bog.

After a most memorable interview in the teachers lounge at the University of Dayton Law school, April 6, 2011

Denny chose to sign the program on a page containing two quotes that remain relevant today:

"If your not part of the solution, you're part of the problem"
— *Eldridge Cleaver*

&

"He who isn't busy being born, is busy dying."
— *Bob Dylan*

denny greene
SHA-NA-NA

In 2011, after another winter down south raising awareness and funds for the graceful quadrupeds we so love, Linda and I decided to take the I-75 home from Tampa to Vermont via Oxford, Ohio. The plan was to stop at Miami University, my alma mater, to visit the adjacent grave-sites of John Weigel and Milton White, then head over to the University of Dayton, where we would try a cold call on Dennis Greene, one of the original members of the retro do-whop group Sha-Na-Na. Dennis is a Professor of Entertainment Law whom I had corresponded with over the years via e-mail but who I could never quite nail down for a formal meet- up. So, as long as Linda and I were in the area, we decided, why not give it a shot. My dad had a saying, " One of two things can happen; something or nothing."

We arrived on the Dayton campus around 11 am and found the law school building. Classes were in full session but the glass atrium lobby was quiet. We checked in at the main office and the secretary's schedule revealed that Professor Greene's class would be letting out any minute; what a break. We could hear the commotion through the windows behind us as hundreds of Dennis' students exited the adjacent lecture hall and surrounded their celebrity teacher in a cult-like fashion so reminiscent of back-stage. Our fearless secretary worked her way into the center of the fray and got Dennis' attention long enough to explain our mission. Dennis swung around with determination and extended his hand; at that moment I knew we had made the right decision. "Hang tight for a bit and I'll see if we can find someplace to talk." I thanked our secretarial assistant for her efforts. As the lobby slowly emptied, Professor Greene suggested that we go to the faculty lounge upstairs, aware that it would offer a conducive environment for the Project. Dennis had two hours before his next class and graciously gave us half. It was one of the most revealing Woodstock Program Project interviews we have ever done.

Dennis, who had spent summers growing up in Harlem singing in street theater groups, advanced his talents at Columbia University by joining the student a Capella group there called The Kingsmen. With only two official school- sponsored gigs a year, and the school administration worried about radical left leaning anarchists seizing Columbia for their anti-Vietnam agenda, the Kingsmen were stuck doing occasional campus appearances singing Broadway show themes and traditional holiday classics. The breakaway moment came when the guys decided to grease back their hair, roll up the sleeves on their T-shirts and do a gig in the school cafeteria. The students liked it so much the group borrowed some costumes from a friend who worked on Broadway (the "Bye, Bye, Birdie" wardrobe was available) and put together a regular show at Columbia they called The Glory that was Grease.

Dennis explains that he was the only member of the group that had any formal dance experience so the choreography fell mostly on his shoulders. By the spring of 1969 the reconfigured Kingsmen had outgrown their school cafeteria. It was time to take the show on the road. The piano player, Joe Wilkin, was the only group member with a car. He and the bass singer, Alan Cooper, teamed up and with a list of clubs in hand, went door to door hoping for an audition. At the last club on their list they got their break. Steve Paul's "The Scene" in the Hell's Kitchen section of New York's west side was a hangout for promoters and rising stars including Jimi Hendrix. In the two weeks that Dennis Greene and friends, now Sha-Na-Na, played The Scene, they landed a record deal, a stint at the Fillmore East and thanks to Jimi Hendrix, a spot on stage at Woodstock.

Early on the morning of Sunday, August 15th, 1969 a limousine picked up Dennis and fellow band member Joe Powell along with Joe Cocker and two members of his group and drove them to a wooded clearing in the woods near Monticello. They were dropped off alone in a location completely unknown to them and told to wait here. "Get out," was the directive given. Dennis recalls the frightfulness of the moment. Some ten minutes into their abandonment and in a scene straight of a Vietnam War documentary, an army helicopter suddenly breaks the silence and drops into the clearing before them. Dennis' teaching skills are on display as he describes for us in vivid detail what went through his mind during that five minute, first ever, helicopter ride over Woodstock. As the copter swung out over the hillside surrounding the concert and settled in across the road and behind the stage, Dennis recalls being drawn to the crowd. "I was struck by the shear magnitude and scope of the event and the power of the people," he relates. He spent most of the morning walking among them sharing their experiences as a casual observer and would, later the same day, do it again with his close friend Gail. Dennis would not elaborate on Gail.

Since Sha-Na-Na was a last minute addition to the Woodstock roster and did not have a dedicated page in the Program. Dennis flipped through and found a page hitherto unsigned labeled "the hard rain's already falling," illustrating a block printed fisted glove and containing these two poignant messages:

I handed Dennis a ballpoint and he inscribed– To Ron and Linda, Denny Greene, Sha-na-na, "Best of luck with your well researched and comprehensive project!"

Thank you for your insight, Denny Greene.

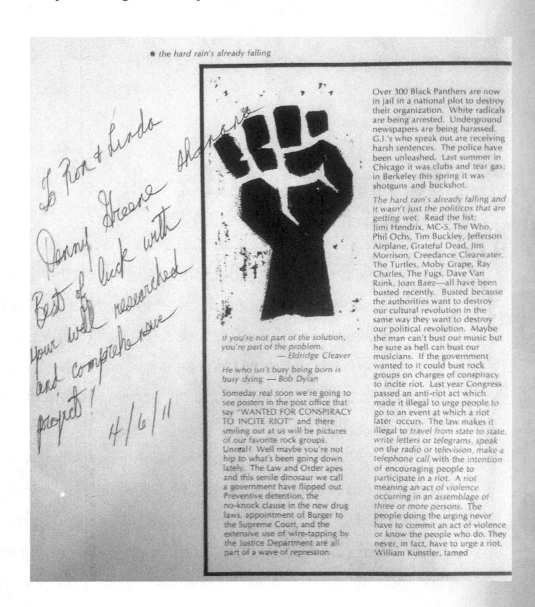

joshua white
THE JOSHUA LIGHT SHOW

Only one artist at Woodstock is listed on the original Program as scheduled to perform on all three days, yet he is probably the least known of our legends. This groundbreaking visual artist's work has probably been seen by more of us than most of his Yasgur's Farm veterans and his accomplishments since are impressive.

Joshua White grew up in Greenwich Village and was schooled at the famous Red School House before enrolling at Carnegie Tech for theater and design. It was during his subsequent years at U.S.C. he was introduced to the cutting edge film technology that became the cornerstone of the liquid, psychedelic, counter-culture, mind altering, metamorphosis for a generation. Joshua White perfected his medium back home in New York and in 1968 struck gold with the opening of Bill Graham's Fillmore East on Manhattan's lower east side. The Joshua Light Show became the official resident stage set for Janis Joplin, The Grateful Dead, Jefferson Airplane, The Doors, The Who and Jimi Hendrix. It was this relationship that led to Woodstock Ventures hiring the amazing Joshua White to create the liquid light backdrop for one of the largest stages ever built to date for an outdoor concert.

I first contacted Josh by e-mail. Our own schedule brought Linda and me through New York, post winter in Florida, the year I began working on this manuscript. Joshua was skeptical, but in his own words, "You sealed the deal when you invited me to join you for a private tour of The MET!" For Josh, the Woodstock Program Project T-shirt alone was not a closer. I had to up the ante and as it turned out, Linda and I had been courting our dear friend, sculptor and ornamental plaster artist David Flaharty for some time to show us the newest restoration work he had done at The Metropolitan Museum of Art. Our good friend Andy Singer from New Jersey was in and when we made our annual stop at David's in Pennsylvania, he said "Yes." It was a date. "Let's meet at noon, right inside the main entrance," I naively suggested, forgetting that almost everyday at The MET is like an episode of "Sex in the City." Good thing we all had cell phones.

After lunch in the museum's café, David took us all on a most splendid private walking tour of his intricate and elegant ornamental craftsmanship which adorns much of the American Wing. The ceiling of the Frank Lloyd Wright room, the many corbels, medallions and friezes that give period authenticity to the maze of 18th, 19th and 20th century furnishings and historic space recreations and too, the rosettes and runs of finish trim that make up the famous Tiffany window displays, are all David's creations. Two hours in, Joshua made some phone calls and moved his schedule back. The hour or so he had planned for the experience was extended to almost four and it wasn't until the last 20 minutes that we addressed the interview and Woodstock Project.

David, Linda, Brigid (Joshua's lifelong friend) and Andy went off on their own as Joshua and I sat down in the cavernous courtyard entry to the museum's American Wing and talked Joshua Light Show, 1969.

"I was only 26 when Woodstock took place but I can tell you that the New York perspective was more disciplined than San Francisco's." I interpreted this to mean that the "Free Love" was somehow free-er and the drugs more pervasive on the coast where it all began. Joshua White, the artist, accepted the challenge of projecting his creations on an enormous outdoor screen even though, as he explains, "Bill Graham was not exactly thrilled with the whole mega-concert idea himself.

"I arrived at Yasgur's Farm on Monday morning, August 11th, before the stage construction had even begun, to meet with Michael (Lang). My friend Shelley Levin and I drove up and back together. The Earth-Lite Players, who were living in our Monticello motel, were called upon numerous times to help push our car out of the mud as the concert stage came together and seven tons of equipment and a bunch of sour hippies began converging on Bethel, New York. David's Pot Belly catered the backstage meals as our team of six or seven lightshow technicians performed until Saturday night when," according to Josh, "our backdrop projection screen was cut down by the Woodstock stage crew to use as cover for the musical equipment, during one of the worst thunderstorms of the weekend."
Joshua and Shelley returned to Manhattan on Sunday afternoon having been unable to do the Joshua Light Show for The Band, Johnny Winter, Crosby Stills and Nash or The Butterfield Blues Band. But just as significant to this book's storyline is Josh having left before the delivery truck carrying the Woodstock Programs finally made it to it's backstage drop zone.

The only semblance of my quarter century-long quest that I had with me for our day at The MET, was an early typewriter-written cover page for this future manuscript. In the center of the 81/2 X 11 inch white bond page are type-written the words "CHASING WOODSTOCK," copyright 2010, Ronald Evans, all rights reserved. Josh signed the page and drew an illuminated light bulb below his name in a style that was remarkably similar to the F.B. Modell illustrations in my uncle Milton White's books and New Yorker Magazine articles. Then it hit me. No way. Yes Way!

My mother's maiden name was White. Her parents, Albert and Rose, were reassigned American names when they came through Ellis Island. The literal interpretation of Bleiweiss was White. The same turned out to be true for Josh. Holy Crap, we're cousins! I looked at Joshua and suddenly realized that he even looked like most of the men on my mother's side. What can I say Josh, you don't plan these things, but it sure is nice to have such talent in the family.

There is a personal genealogical irony associated with the White narrative. A kind of genotypic flaw, call it a core conserved DNA characteristic that I always jokingly referred to as "The Eckstein Gene," seemed to conserve almost every member of my father's side of the family. Immediate aunts, uncles and cousins alike all exhibited inescapable solipsistic hubris. The Whites were never good enough for the Ecksteins. I know now that this was a classic case of a phenotypic inferiority/superiority complex. Simply put, mom's family turned out to be kind, generous, creative intellectuals and dad's a bunch of self-promoting, arrogant, megalomaniacs. Boy, am I glad I got a predominance of mother's genes!

In case you doubt my earlier claim that most of you know Joshua White's artistry, here is a partial list of his work since Woodstock:

- Joshua created the legendary party scenes in both John Schlisinger's Academy Award winning movie, Midnight Cowboy and Bette Midler's, The Rose.
- He has produced and directed a range of classic TV shows including Seinfeld, The Jerry Lewis Telethon, Max Headroom and Inside the Actors Studio.

- Joshua Light Show has performed at Lincoln Center, Carnegie Hall and Tanglewood.
- JLS has been featured in the exhibition Visual Music organized by The Hirschhorn Museum, Washington, D.C.
- The Tate Museum/Liverpool included JLS in their Summer of Love exhibition in 2006 followed by an engagement at The Whitney.

During the summer of 2012, I was invited to attend the Vermont Writers Conference held along the shore of the remote inter-mountain fresh water Tinmouth Lake, a short drive from our grist mill home. The first discipline exercise we were given was "You've got three minutes to compose a poem." The idea was to free our minds and let the thought just flow. I would like to dedicate what flowed out, to my uncle Milton White who worked assiduously during my sophomore year at Miami University to get me through the basics of English Literature, while maintaining his own vigorous schedule of publishing and educating, and to cousin Joshua.

"Seven Tons of Equipment and a Bunch of Sour Hippies"
a poem by Ron Evans

I arrived on Monday morning, fore the stage was built below
Though the weather seemed submissive, it was not to be foretold
Mine was meant to bring white light
To a field of loving souls
But possessing Frisco's memories would abrogate my goals
I drank; I smoked for what seemed like days when Pot Belly came to fill the void
The Garden will soon be re-planted and
the sound of a generation will fill this field of dreams.
For three days in August, seven tons of liquid light and a half a million hippies will draw sensory enlightenment from my minds eye…
Let it flow

Author's note: To Milton White, thank you for the inspiration.

"Boola, Boola, Babe Ruth and a jug of whisky sours" —*From the novel A Yale Man*
Doubleday Publishing.

Cousin Joshua and friend Brigid pose
with master craftsman and sculptor, David
Flaharty at the Frank Lloyd Wright room
of the Metropolitan Museum of Art. David
installed the ceiling ornamentation here for
the most recent American Wing restoration.

Josh and I post signing and interview in the
MET's courtyard.

Joshua and Michael Lang: courtesy of
Joshua White.

Stephanie's antique store in Fort Anne, New York.

the safka soliloquy

It's simple. From the moment I heard "Candles in the Rain" and saw the adorable Melanie for the first time, I was smitten. By the time I got to meet her at Yasgur's Farm in '94 she had lost her girlish figure but had passed on the genetic traits to her two daughters who by then had started their own singing group, called "Safka". It was Déjà vu. It was Smitten, Part II. The kids were gorgeous and talented; what's not to like?

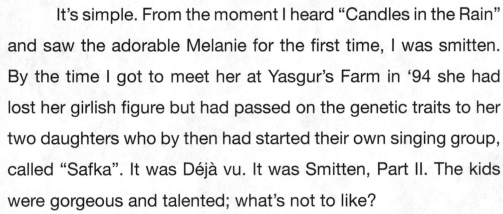

The years moved on and so did Melanie. Our winters in Florida put us only minutes away from Safety Harbor, the address that she had given me to send the extra Woodstock Program T-shirts, but my appreciation for celebrity privacy prevented my inviting additional inter-action between us. Then the darnedest thing happened.

After "Irene," the 2011 hurricane that struck Vermont with life-changing flood waters, Linda and I were hard pressed to find 6 over 6 window sashes from the 1800's that would replace those carried down stream from the first floor of our Grist Mill home. As a last resort we decided to try the Whitehall and Fort Ann, New York antique shops we had passed by for decades. I remembered seeing old window frames standing up in the shop's backyard.

Our first stop in Whitehall was closed for the day but we struck gold at the Fort Ann Antique Center with more than a half dozen fair to good condition sashes of equal dimension for our needs. All would need new glass, glazing and a fresh coat of paint, but at $10.00 each they were the right price for our budget.

We left the windows in a neat line out back and went inside to work out a final cost with the proprietor when I noticed a stack of vinyl LP's on the floor. You know that I can't pass up an opportunity to peruse through classic albums in the most unexpected places in search of a rare find. I still hold out hopes of discovering a mint condition Beatles "Dismemberment" album for $5.00! As Steven Tyler says, "Dream On." But as I flipped through the albums in Fort Ann, I unearthed a find almost as wonderful. Interspersed among the junk vinyl I found not one or two but six Melanie albums in mint and mint minus condition, all of which I needed to round out my Melanie LP library. With concealed excitement I approached the checkout counter. "I've never seen so many Melanie albums in one place," I explained to the shop attendant. Then I noticed a Melanie concert poster hanging high up on the wall behind the counter. "Does someone here have a connection with Melanie?" I inquired. "Well actually, Yes," she answered shyly. "The shop is owned by Stephanie Safka, Melanie's sister! These are from her personal collection." Sold, for $3.99 each.

All those years spent trying to connect with Melanie the Woodstock legend and it turns out that her younger sister lives less than 20 minutes away and owns a shop Linda and I have admired and visited time and again. I took Stephanie's business card and called back with a request for an interview, not about "Ms. M." but about "Growing up Safka." Stephanie consented and on Friday morning, July 13th, 2012, I drove over to Fort Ann, pad and pen in tow.

Stephanie's Fort Ann Antique Shop is located in a 19th century historic three story brick building at the corner of Rte 4 and 149, a twenty minute drive east of Lake George, New York.* We hung out near the antique cash register below the Melanie Concert Poster as I began by recounting the Album story and the irony of having missed the clues before. "Tell me your story," I proposed. "What was it like for you growing up Safka?" I wanted this to be all Stephanie.

Both she and older sister Melanie were born in Astoria Queens but grew up in New Jersey in the '50's and '60's with their mother Polly, an accomplished jazz singer. By the time Melanie was old enough to enroll in New York City's American Academy of Arts, her mom had already recorded several albums of her own and according to Stephanie, older sister Melanie knew what she wanted and even as a child pursued her destiny with the "passion and flame" needed to succeed in the business. In Stephanie's own words, "The more I saw, the less I wanted to be an entertainer. When you see Tim Hardin asking for a needle backstage or Bob Dylan arrogantly ordering people around, you think this is not my cup of tea."

Instead, Stephanie left home as a teenager and eventually landed in upstate New York where, as a passionate advocate for environmental regulation and for controlling one's own destiny, she gave birth to the Recycling Movement in Washington County. By finding outlets for more than two-dozen previously un-recycled products, Stephanie helped remove tons of waste from the local landfills and raise awareness in her community.

Stephanie was only 14 years old when she, Melanie and their Aunt Jeanie went to Yasgur's Farm and her sister's career was launched. We had to break from our interview as tears overcame her when she spoke of being Aunt Stephanie to Leilah, Jeordie, Beau and the family dynamics and distances between them. I didn't pry.

I salute you Stephanie and hope that you receive the recognition and support that is due you for your work next door and please give my regards to M and the kids. I think of you every time I play a Melanie album.

Finding the prized Melanie LP's and Mill windows. One stop shopping!

just pen pals

If I hadn't lived it, I wouldn't have believed it either, but in the mid and late sixties, when a contemporary song was released in America, it seemed to be released first in the mid-west; I'm guessing for test market reasons. Middle and high school age brother Ken would begin hearing the same songs two to three weeks later, making big brother Ron his embedded prognosticator of future hit songs. In the hay day of the Beatles, Rolling Stones, Psychedelic and Bubble Gum, I would call home with weekly reports of what was playing on the radio here and he would inform his closest friends back home what was coming. Sure enough, like a crystal ball right on schedule, there they were.

The big downside to this one way street was that if a band from say the northeast hadn't been discovered nationally and did not venture beyond that market area, I too, was in the dark. Such was the case with a band from Boston that toured exclusively in New England, New York and New Jersey during the lead up to Woodstock.

Brothers Jonathan and Daniel Cole attended Northfield Mount Hermon Prep together before stints at the Boston Museum School and Bard College respectively. A subsequent opportunity to showcase their music before a local music management entrepreneur named Ray Paret brought keyboardist Phil Thayer, guitarist Norm Rogers and percussionist Roger North into the line-up who would come to be named for the bands creative penmanship.

Pre-dating the legendary New England Rock bands like Aerosmith, Boston and Phish, "Quill" had the experimental sound anchored in classical training that landed them a gig at guess where? Once again, Steve Paul's "The Scene" in New York City played a pivotal role for the final Woodstock roster you now know as the Original Woodstock Program. It was here too, that Quill would get to jam with Jimi Hendrix and Stephen Stills in the presence of Michael Lang that landed them an invitation to come to Yasgur's Farms.

Earlier pre-web efforts on my part to find Quill had ended in frustration and to be perfectly honest, with my limited resources, I had bigger fish to fry. I simply set Quill aside. Armed now with a hand-me-down Apple G4 laptop and access to my neighbors wifi, a renewed effort led me to the salient innovator and former Quill drummer Roger North who forwarded my query to founder and lead singer Dan Cole.

In a January 2014 phone interview, the band's outspoken and personable singer/guitarist laid out in great detail the dynamics surrounding Quill's anticipated appearance at Woodstock. "We became the official PR band for Woodstock Ventures in the lead up to August 15th 1969. Three to four nights a week prior to the concert we would play venues nearby the newly secured lower Catskill Yasgur's Farm". Dan explains. Local theaters and bars were offered free Quill appearances to help gain acceptance of a music genre considered alien to many in the small upstate farming communities around Bethel. "They had us playing everything from old folks homes to gatherings for site workers to local Grange halls but, the one that stands out in my minds eye is the show we were booked to do at the Beacon Hospital for the Criminally Insane". he continues, " They set us up in a steel cage between two rooms of inmates. When things got heated and a few of the inmates flipped out, we were ushered to safety by armed guards. It was a gig I will never forget. "Woodstock was truly a once in a lifetime opportunity, he laments. Looking back, Dan has a clear and realistic sentiment of Quill's Saturday afternoon performance at Yasgur's Farm.

Following Woodstock, Ahmet Ertegun, Head of Atlantic Records signed Quill and promptly released what turned out to be their only album on the Cotillion label. Having missed being featured on the sound-track album for what was claimed to be technical difficulties, sales fell far short of expectations. Quill's artists moved on to individual pursuits. Brother Jonathan started up a solar energy firm and now lives in Hawaii. Roger North went on to invent the famous North Drum Set, still prized by those lucky enough to own one. After Woodstock, Dan helped produce Joe Cocker's back-up band before taking on a V.P. position with Sony Music, working with TV networks back in the 1990's. "I travelled the world with Sony for a couple of years. I realized it was making me a wealthy but stressed out family man." Dan, decided that his family and his health were his priorities and now plays guitar with the Freak Mountain Ramblers in and around the Portland, Oregon area, occasionally reuniting with Quill veteran Roger North. I can't help but think too, that Dan made a sound judgement call when, back in the 70's, he traded a Who poster he had collected for an even rarer "mirrored" original Woodstock poster.

I hope to catch up to Dan and Roger for the first time in person during a west coast book tour for Chasing Woodstock. Here's the deal - I'll show them The Program if they'll show me their artistry. After all those years wondering where that 60's (pen) stroke of genius Quill vanished to, it turns out that guitarist Norm Rogers had, for some 25 years, been living about a one hour drive from Linda and me, in Brattleboro, Vermont. He passed away on July 9th, 2011.

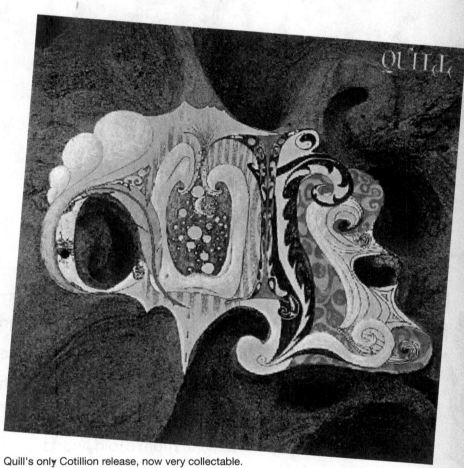

Quill's only Cotillion release, now very collectable.

Eva at work in Rutland, Vermont.

eva's secret

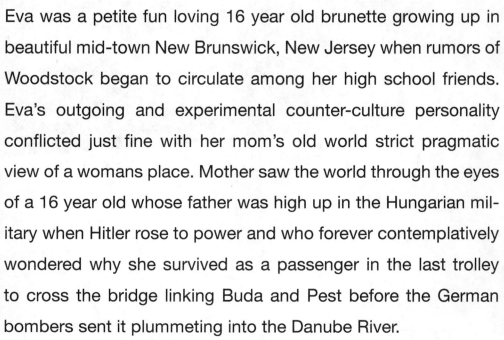

Eva was a petite fun loving 16 year old brunette growing up in beautiful mid-town New Brunswick, New Jersey when rumors of Woodstock began to circulate among her high school friends. Eva's outgoing and experimental counter-culture personality conflicted just fine with her mom's old world strict pragmatic view of a womans place. Mother saw the world through the eyes of a 16 year old whose father was high up in the Hungarian military when Hitler rose to power and who forever contemplatively wondered why she survived as a passenger in the last trolley to cross the bridge linking Buda and Pest before the German bombers sent it plummeting into the Danube River.

Eva had no such past to contend with. Hers was a world of

R.J. Youngs Clothing, Barton's Candy and Woolworths department stores. Her two story, picket fenced, white brick and azalea adorned home on Mason Avenue was just blocks from the neighborhood park. She and her girlfriends could walk there and to school without a care. "My best friend's mom was my mom's best friend," Eva explained. "We were inseparable."

Eva's mom was so strict that she would not let her go outside in jeans – tight fitting or otherwise. Young ladies wore dresses- mom insisted. But this was 1969 and for Eva the lure of long hair, brightly colored beads and bell-bottom jeans was too hard to resist. "I would stuff my flower child hippie wear into my giant red, white and blue fringed bag and change at my girlfriend's house. My friend's mom was in on the whole deception," Eva admitted.

"When school let out for summer I was expected to get a job and carry my weight at home. Someone knew someone who knew that the in-town Ritz Diner on George Avenue needed help. They gave me a job for the summer but it had to be off the books. I was only 16, legal was 17!" she professes.

Eva's secrets were starting to pile up. This "sweet little sixteen" hippie chick was not quite as sweet as mom thought. She had already experimented a nip with alcohol and was getting off on Acapulco Gold when the summer waitressing thing took off. "I could walk to work and the money was good" admits Eva. She got some regular customers, mostly at lunch time. You know the scene. Friends drop in and locals come and go, but that year one customer caught Eva's eye. He was tall and thin with dark hair, probably in his early twenties and he always asked to sit in her section. He was almost never alone and those who accompanied him at lunch were "mostly suits. "He was well dressed and charming," Eva remembers. "A good tipper." Then in early August, Mr. Charming made Eva an offer she couldn't refuse. "Me and a few friends are going to a concert next weekend and we have an extra ticket. Would you like to come?" Eva needed some time to weigh her options. "Are you coming in tomorrow?" she asked. "Of course." "I'll let you know then," she proposed.

It would have been easy for our Eva to "just say no" to a first date with Mr. Charming but then, this was 1969 and our girl was ready to take that quantum leap into women's liberation-ville: all she needed were some accomplices to keep the secret from mom. She hatched her plan on the walk home and stopped at her friend's house to "get our story straight."

"Mom must never know." It would take a coordinated effort to pull off such a deception. Eva's master plan was brilliant and I'm sure never thought of before by any 16 year-old girl. "I would be staying at Jill's house for the weekend," she proposed. A true stroke of genius. OK, maybe not, but when Jill's mom agreed to cover for our disreputably charming protagonist, Eva was in like flint.

"Yes, I'll go," she told her date the following day. "There are six others coming with us," he informed her. "I'll pick you up here on Friday afternoon after work. Bring whatever you'll need for a couple of days: we're going to Woodstock!"

Our daring little Eva was embarking on her very first date and it was with a guy maybe ten years her senior which, as you may recall, is like the old dude to a 16 year old. She trusted this guy intuitively and figured that, if push came to shove, there would be a few thousand other kids to help rescue her. So the plan was set. There would be no turning back as Friday's workday ended and her date arrived right on time. "We'll be meeting the others at my place for the trip up," he explained. "We're all travelling together." For just a moment Eva's excitement was breached by the prospect that she and her apparently clueless date and his friendly suits would end up spending the weekend stuck in the endless traffic jam that was all over the local news. "As long as we had some good weed with us I was OK with whatever happened," Eva admits.

Eva's pick up ride from work only lasted 20 minutes. Her date pulled his car up to a set of steel gates, entered a code and made his way into the rear of one of the largest corporate headquarters our girl had ever seen. "Oh Wow, what are we doing here?" she asked. "It's the family business" he insisted. "We'll be leaving shortly" and before he could get the rest of the details out, the car swung around the back of the building and sitting right smack in the middle of the parking lot was the most beautiful pure white helicopter Eva had ever seen,   awaiting her arrival. You can't make this stuff up. Eva Tarnoczy's first date was in a corporate helicopter from the back lot of the Johnson & Johnson World headquarters in New Jersey to back stage at Yasgur's farm on Friday afternoon, August the 15th,1969, landing somewhere in between Joan Baez and Ravi Shankar.

Were you there? Do you remember seeing the big white helicopter coming in for a landing? Or did everything look like a big white helicopter to you that day? Arlo tells of being so stoned that he fell through a big hole in the stage and the next thing he recalls is being magically levitated back up to the microphone for his first set.

The Johnson & Johnson kids got to Yasgur's Farm just in time to hear Melanie, Arlo and the crowd-pleasing soprano, Ms. Baez. But of all the acts scheduled for that historic weekend it was Country Joe & the Fish that Eva wanted to hear most. She and her fellow white bird travellers would have to bunk in under blankets and tarps that were no match for the night-time thunderstorms and resulting mud. "I remember waking up cold and wet but when Joe McDonald took the stage it was all just fine," she insists. By the time Santana finished Soul Sacrifice, our Eva started feeling that guilt that moms do so well. Has mom found out? Will I be disowned?

By late Saturday it was agreed that wet, cold and hungry was no match for lunch at The Ritz Diner. The kids knew that "a change was gonna come" and that they would be "leavin this town" before Canned Heat did. No long walks home for our first date vixen from New Brunswick. After all, this was a family owned company!

Eva wouldn't tell me if she slept alone that night on Yasgur's Farm but she did reveal the best and most innocent of secrets during our interview. When she got back to Jill's house she discovered that the plan had actually worked. "Your mom has no idea where you've been." Jill was amazed to report. Eva's Woodstock secret was safe.

"So when did your mom finally find out about your Woodstock date?" I asked as our interview came to a close. A look of apprehension and guilt flowed over Eva's face "Well...never," she blushed. "Are you telling me that your mother still does not know you went to Woodstock?" I bemoaned. "That's right, she's 93 years old and she must never know," Eva insists. "But she may find out when she reads this book," I suggested, just to cover my own ass. Eva's response: "she will never see your book. If she ever found out, she would never forgive me." So I'm trusting all of you to help me keep Eva's secret. I gave her my word that I would never tell.

Mother, right, and daughter share a brew at the Long Trail Brewery in Bridgewater, Vermont, circa 2003.

Swing dance artist (Country Joe & the Fish) Mark Kapner.

swinging out with mark kapner
COUNTRY JOE & THE FISH

Chasing down Country Joe & the Fish' Woodstock keyboardist, Mark Kapner was no easy task.

It all started back in 2011 when I found out that Mark, who grew up in New England but has spent most of his life since Woodstock living in California style, still maintained a connection with his roots in neighboring New Hampshire. Mark had developed a keen awareness of the world around him and insisted on getting the most out of every day. Instead of running from the past, he had found peace in embracing it, bringing it full circle along with his youthful maturity. To that end, Mark had re-discovered the 21st century variation of a

20th century dance form known as the Lindy Hop. Todays version 'Swing Dancing' attracts hundreds of dedicated followers to Camp Wicosuta in New Hampshire every August for an event that Mark and his colleages call Swing Out New Hampshire.

My first contact with Fish member Mark Kapner was in July of that year. The plan was to make the two and one half hour mountain pass drive to the camp on the day of Marks arrival. Instead, hurricane Irene struck Vermont the exact same day severing all east/west highways.; another close encounter obviated. The e-mails that followed between us sent a clear message that I wasn't giving up.

After two years of storm rebuilding it was time to give it another try. Mark was already on his way east when he got my call to open another chapter of the Woodstock Program adventure. We set up a pre-noon arrival at the camp and with calm and sunny skys forecast, we arrived on schedule.

Camp Wicosuta is located on the lower western shore of Newfound Lake in the Granite State. It is the ideal setting for young girls from the city to escape from the summer heat and instead, re-create themselves surrounded by mother natures gifts.

At the close of the camps summer season, Mark et. al., begin the arduous task of converting the cafeteria and conference centers into dance halls for their Labor Day weekend extravaganza. We caught up with Mark at the administration building surrounded by immaculately landscaped tennis courts, swimming pools and even a miniature open lattice covered bridge for that ultimate New England experience. He was tall, lean and dressed in jeans and a black T with "Swing Out New Hampshire" emblazened on the front. Marks years since his famous Sunday performance on stage at Woodstock had not diminished his Rock Star appearance. I would have guessed him to be the same age as me but, in fact he was beginning his freshman year at Brown when I was entering my freshman year at Central High. Kapner got right down to business. "So whatta ya got?", he queried. I answered with a question, "Have you ever seen the original concert program from Woodstock?" I got the answer I wanted. "No". "Did you go?" he asked. A "no" answer was returned. Offering up an ever so brief summation of the parents and the hippie van gas story kept Mark focused on the prize and his curiousity peaked. "Well, lets see this thing" he insisted and we were off and running. His initial responses were cynical. "I always hated this psychedelic balloon style of lettering", followed by, "I couldn't understand why they (Woodstock attendees) were sitting around in garbage and mud when they could have been home having sex, listening to their stereos and smoking a joint." You know Ron, we were promised steak and a buffet back stage and all we got was bologna and bread sticks, Oh and champagne of course!"

In an effort to get the mood re-directed, I asked Mark to recall his journey east and getting to Yasgur's Farm. "We flew into New York, picked up a car and drove there on Saturday morning, arriving at the Liberty, Holiday Inn mid-day." He tells us about being stuck at the hotel, "with a very drunk Keith Moon (The Who) while Joe went off to check out the event. I tried to get a chopper ride with this girl I met but they refused to let us on, on Saturday" Mark recounts. But Sunday was a different story. With Joe and the Fish scheduled, the band had no problem getting onboard one of the helicopters for a birdseye preview of their 6:30 pm performance. " I grew up in a camp environment in the northeast so I had a pretty good idea what an impending storm looked like. From a chopper it's even more ominous" he explains. We landed just before things got ugly and by the time the storm passed, the wind swept rain had impregnated much of the stage and its hastily covered electronics. Marks 90 minute performance brought with it concern of being electrocuted and thoughts about sound quality issues. "The instruments were so soaked that the sound came out tinny" he adds. Just about the time the truck carrying the Woodstock Programs made it to the back stage drop zone, Mark, Joe, Barry, Greg and Doug (Country Joe & the Fish) were on their flight back to the hotel."We must have just missed seeing them" he admits. Almost 44 years to the week later, another art tragedy would be rectified.

Linda, Mark and I made our way over to the camp conference center where lunch was being served up to staff and the director offered to include us. Over the buffet-style picnic of lunch meat and salad, Mark shared with us some of his personal ideals, values and impressions: How he lives his life in balance with the forces of nature around and within himself. Before adding his signature next to fellow band member Joe McDonald, Mark opened up to us about his post Woodstock world of swing dancing. "I have had two hip replacements and still I compete", he admits. It has become a big part of who he is today. If you need inspiration, Mark suggests that you check out two classic movies that are guaranteed to get you hooked. The Marx Brothers "A Day at the Races", their 1937 film which also starred Maureen O'Sullivan, the mom of our late friend and fellow artist Patrick Farrow (Mia's brother) and the 1941 Universal Pictures release of H.C. Potter's "Hellzapoppin' ", are in his opinion the best examples of the swing and pre-swing Lindy Hop ever set down on film. But even after his 1970 and '71 tour with Neil Diamond and a long term love affair with swing dance, I came away with the feeling that this rock counter-culture keyboardist whose fame and legacy will forever be linked to "Gimme an F, Gimme a U" would have no trouble picking up the chant once again when and if that time comes.

chapter nine
FINDING THE COST OF FREEDOM OR THE ANSWER

I have now lived 66 years. For someone whose generation is defined as "Post War," I have grown up in a country that, with few exceptions, has been fighting wars all my life. Yet, even as a child and on into young adulthood, it didn't take long to learn that the art of negotiation and reasoned intervention always lead to a more peaceful and beneficial outcome for all parties involved. We're not talking rocket science here; just common sense and a little self control. When a confrontation presented itself, I was usually the one to step in, as a neutral, third party arbitrator and make the case, most often to the individual most upset or emotionally charged, that taking this to the next level was not in THEIR best interest. Look, it's not in my best interest either. Nobody wins. Agree to disagree if we must. Shake hands, don't shake hands; I don't care; crisis averted, period. This, Plan B, always offer a save face option to fighting, only failed to work once in my entire life and by the time that day came, I was old enough and skilled enough to know how to physically defend myself against my confronter. He was a 6' 2", 285 lb. football player at Miami and I was a 5' 10", 160 lb. hippie gymnast with a gregarious, Yankee attitude that had no place on HIS mid-west campus. Within the confinement of our sophomore year dormitory, every attempt to reason with this guy fell on deaf (and dumb) ears. He showed up at my door to "teach me a lesson." For the first time, Plan B was not an option. Schembeckler's Bully had failed to see past his fear to recognize just how strong and agile gymnasts can be. He never bothered me again. The incident would remain a compelling argument to always strive for honest and open dialogue over fear aggression, at all cost.

So, if detente seems so much easier to achieve at the most basic level of human social interaction, and the results, that much more palatable at every level of instinctive behavior, what then is the core intervening variable that stands so firmly in the way of applying the same reason and logic to our everyday discourse? I am about to foray into the most feared subject the world has ever known. The mere mention of this topic evokes contemptuous hostility in the hearts of three quarters of the world's 6.5 billion inhabitants who have grown up under its doctrines. A lifetime of free scientific inquiry and experience has narrowed it down to one and only one, undeniably clear answer: mono-theism.

The case for undeniability seems so concise and overpowering that, were it to be put forth under any other reasoned and rational premise or circumstance, the consequences would be moot; the consensus overwhelming. In a world of religious patriarchs, as pre-ordained by ancient literature, there can be no such consensus. The cycle remains embedded in the fabric of a society through time, purely because the indoctrination begins at birth and it is so much easier to be an obedient follower than a free thinker. I mean come on. When did you " Just said NO!" to the absurd notion that there is a Santa Claus, an Easter Bunny or a Tooth Fairy? At what age did it strike you that you had been lied to your entire childhood. I know a few adults that still believe. Then came the years of religious schooling where you were either taught that you are the chosen people or that everything you do or will do for the rest of your life is or will be sinful, with your only hope for salvation being to beg forgiveness. Either way the results are fear and subrogation followed by exclusivity and separatism. Any hope you may have of breaking free of the dogma will be swiftly dealt with using guilt and/or excommunication. Either way, you're out of The Will.

OK, for the sake of argument, I'm willing to play the devils advocate. Let's say that there actually is an old bearded man in the sky who holds the key to a set of Pearly Gates leading to a cloud laden heaven where all your past friends and relative, who never got along on earth, suddenly await your ascent. When you arrive, are you going to be greeted by 72 virgins, a two thousand year-old exiled and crucified Jewish carpenter or worse yet, all 100 billion former hominids, homo-erectus and Homo-sapiens that have lived and died on the planet in a half million years, give or take? Didn't they all qualify to pass your particular god's entrance exam? Really! If your answer is still yes and the basis for your decision is "Faith," you should probably close this book now and pick one that is, instead, filled with violence, deceit, deception, murder, rape, infant torture, assassination, stoning, and lets not forget the ever present contradictions in verse. Almost any archaic and out of date scripture would do. Before you make your final decision, may I put forth a bold new option? Back in the 16th century, your religion probably concurred with Christianity's position that Copernicus was out to lunch when he postulated that the sun, not the earth, was the center of a heliocentric planetary system. A short time later, in the scheme of things, it probably agreed again with Christianity that Galileo was a heretic for concurring with Copernicus through scientific observations made using his newly devised telescope. He would be jailed for the rest of his life for defying the commonly held Christian theosophy. By the way, the pope and the Vatican did apologize and forgave Galileo for the misunderstanding, in 2010! When one's beliefs are so completely out of touch with the empirical realities of the natural world we inhabit, the only way to salvage control of its multi-trillion dollar empire is to create a parallel reality. Done. See how easy that is. Ah, the wonders of modern technology. Now we can actually see the "Ghost" of Patrick Swayze pass right through Demi Moore. How about that parting of the Red Sea! Did you know that it was the nationwide promotion of that picture, "The Ten Commandments," back in 1958, that started the whole erection (am I still allowed to use that word?) of cast Ten Commandment monuments in public parks and civic sites throughout the U.S.? One's religious beliefs and affiliations were firmly ensconced and insured in the Constitutional separation of church and state affairs for almost 200 years until the Eisenhower administration breached the public trust and embraced the official use of the motto "In God We Trust" on legal tender in America for the first time. Eisenhower's fear of an autonomous and over-reaching military/industrial machine in tandem with the inclusion of a hitherto personal religious enterprise into the public discourse, had re-branded what had been America's greatest constitutional strength, into it's most self destructive weakness. America, at the start of the 21st century, is in a psychological and systemic funk, not only because of a sudden and unexpected economic downturn, but because it is entrapped in it's own "spiritual" Black Hole of Dark Energy, without the fortitude to challenge it's causal host. Back in 2002 when friends gathered to discuss the impending Iraq invasion, I raised the question of W's deeply fundamental Christian belief system as a possible motivation. I never forgot the response I received, mostly by my Christian friends. "You're probably correct, but don't EVER expect to have or hear that discussion in this country." It was simply too sensitive to talk about, I was told. The evidence, however, was everywhere. From the exclusionary faith based prayer breakfasts in the White House, to K Street, to Christian hazing, inculcation and prosthelization condoned and encouraged by a 90% Christian military, to the often secret funneling of public funds to religious institutions, to the outlandish proliferation of tax exempt churches and Supreme Court-protected pseudo-personhood, it is impossible to ignore the overwhelming evidence before us. For too long, ignore it we have, with the hope that the next election cycle would put us back on the road to a freedom FROM religion. Having fought for religious independence from this most basic dynamic, our founders established as a cornerstone to a new world order, one that placed our human moral and ethical standards above all others. In America, freedom from religion also guaranteed freedom for religion, as long as the respect remained mutual. But, how mutual is that respect today when, according to Ryan Cragun, assistant professor of Sociology at the University of Tampa, the total cost of religious tax exemptions to the U.S. Treasury is estimated at $71 billion annually.* My fellow citizens, I contend that the very foundation of our country's greatness has been so morally corrupted and theosophized, that we now stoop to fighting in the same gutters, around the globe, that we so proudly held ourselves, for two centuries, at greater superintendence. In this 21st century, no less so than in others that have passed and will follow, our minds, our common bonds and our technology are our greatest assets; if we can find the fortitude to free them, we free ourselves. Do not be deceived. Make no mistake, deceit and deception are all around you. I remind you that, just as "W" was leaving office and the Big Three auto makers were about to get bailed out, the president of General Motors was asked how long it would take for G.M. to develop a 70 mile per gallon car. His deliberate and deceitful answer was 7 to 10 years. Months later, Japan announced that they had produced one. Rent the movie "Who Killed the Electric Car" if you're in doubt. To add insult to injury, under the Obama administration's oversight, in 2008, G.M. was once again given a challenge: design a 100 mile per gallon car. Their pedantic answer this time: 10 years. Three years later, VW announced that they not only succeeded at inventing the 100 m.p.g. vehicle, they had super-ceded the goal and had created a 257 mile per gallon car. To further demoralize the formerly great land of opportunity, the new VW would sell brand new for the U.S. equivalent price of $600.00.

Do not think for one minute that the progressive ideology in our land of "liberty and justice for all" and "of the people, by the people and for the people" hasn't been hijacked by the privileged 1%. Let me tell you a story about a home that my dad and I engineered back in 1979 that was completely fossil fuel free and "miraculously" self-sufficient. Moreover, it was of conventional construction and inexpensive to build. It was indeed, the first hybrid home in the state of Connecticut and was so revolutionary it was featured in Popular Mechanics Magazine.* Our secret ingredient in the design was a NASA inspired insulation, so advanced that 3 inches had an R-value of 70 (equal to 28" of fiberglass). That's right, a handful of this stuff was completely impermeable to hot and cold. It was, in fact, the world's most perfect insulation and had it been allowed to be brought to market, would have guaranteed

America's ecological and financial security for generations. Think about it; you would have been heating your home for the past 30 years with nothing more than the solar collectors on your roof and probably a candle in every room! You can't make this stuff up. The product was called "Perlite" and the patent was owned by Danial K Dunn, Kankakee, Illinois. Patent # 4000241. Don't talk to me of that "land of the free or liberty and justice for all" bull shit! I believe the patent for this revolutionary technology was obtained by its most fervent corporate competitor and locked in a vault. Corporate greed, fueled by a myth-based dogma that condones misguided priorities and pseudo-realities, gives the privileged among us the excuse necessary to create a self-promoting and untouchable parallel universe. When the methods employed to accomplish this systemic corruption are so entrenched in a society, that its citizens are willing to vote against the very issues that benefit them most, well then, " Houston, we have a problem." How is this so easily accomplished? Keep everyone busy in virtual space playing mindless games, racking up bogus friends or meaningless on-line points or simply requiring them to now do, themselves, all the things they used to go to experts (neighbors whom you trusted and who were personally responsible for their actions) to do. If the masses are busy just trying to keep from drowning and the antidote for the cure is religious false hope, maybe they won't notice that the captain has left the sinking ship and has relocated to his own private tropical island paradise. I am flabbergasted that this deception still endures after thousands of years. Promise the flock eternal bliss or an afterlife of virginal, vaginal, vitriol, and they'll hasten their own demise to acquire it. The unfortunate consequence of this brutal deception is that if one is convinced that the value of a next life is significantly higher than the current one, what motivation will remain to attach any real value to, what just might be, the only life you'll ever experience? Therein lies the core issue that I've been told I cannot talk about. What is so bad about "living in peace, then resting in peace? I'd opt for eternal rest any day over, forever with some of the members of my biological family. Tell me you can't relate? It's simply easier to go along with the old traditions and demagoguery than it is to seek the perceived alienation of empirical truth and knowledge. You will be encouraged to know, however, that in 21st century America, though less prolific than in almost all the rest of the developed world, the acceptance and advancement of non-mono-theistic and non-religious social structure is the single fastest growing human life philosophy. It is estimated that, in the U.S. alone, some 40 million people have made world peace and love, without super-natural mythology, a life changing world- view.

If you are one of the tens of millions who didn't know that there are alternatives to false hope, or that morality is a human value, not a gift from the supernatural, here are a few sites and subjects you may wish to explore: Francis Ellingwood Abbot, John Dewey, Francois Marie Arouet, Baruch Spinoza, Claude Adrien Helvetius, Robert Greene Ingersoll, Dr. Spencer Wells (Journey of Man, 2003 and The Human Family Tree, 2009, film documentaries), Christoper Hitchens, Bertrand Russell, Buddhism, Secular Humanism.org. A web search will lead you on a journey of self-gratification, non-antidisestablishmenterianism (I always wanted to use that word in print), and most of all, a new synaptic eupraxsophy that hasn't been felt since Woodstock; had we only known. The good news; it's never too late.

You'll have to keep an open mind and be willing to let go of a lifetime of misinformation and indoctrination, but along the way you'll meet a world of like-minded explorers who, just like you, are discovering that the chase is so worth the effort. My parents instilled in me some very powerful, yet painfully simple, life lessons. The "something or nothing" thing best exemplifies this point, for who can argue against its basic logic. Yet the psychology behind its simple dynamic is so very cogent. Here's one you are probably familiar with; "Knowledge is power." Seek empirical reason and knowledge alone. You'll know it when you find it. It is universally verifiable and tested again and again over time. Albert Einstein's Theory of Relativity and Charles Darwin's Theory of Evolution have both passed this test of empirical truth for generations (including the discovery of Facilitated Variation), yet, blind faith clings hopelessly to delusion and a volume of contradictory writings that were fabricated 100 years after the events, they claim so manifestly to portray, would have occurred. It is no wonder that the books of Mark and John cannot agree on when, where or how their God was born. Theologians do agree on one thing, however. Historical evidence abounds that most of Christianity's story line was plagiarized from earlier pagan, Indian and Persian scripture. Virgin births, Guiding Stars, Resurrections and Mangers were already popular for hundreds of years before Jesus, in the forms of Mithra, Zoroaster, Krishna and Buddha. Look, the bottom line here is that this is a conflict that nobody wins. We know this because no other single enterprise has, for two thousand years or more, been responsible for as much human death and suffering, worldwide, as organized religion. There isn't even a close second.

I am not proposing the eradication of religion. One would be equally delusional to believe the potentiality of the premise. Woodstock worked for many serendipitous reasons but at the top of the list is the fact that overt, denominational religious proselytization was not present. Woodstock almost didn't work, solely because religiously based fear and hatred played into the local political process, nearly terminating the permitting of the event before it began. My Chase has offered me many exclusive interviews with people within the workings and proximity of Yasgur's Farm in Bethel, New York where the famous concert was held. One such interview was with Clara Joyner, the co-owner of the Bethel Store on Rte 17B , just 1 mile from the stage. Richard and Clara Joyner's small, pillared, family owned, combination post office, gas station and country store was ground zero for last stop supplies before the final leg of the trek to the site. The family had been so traumatized by Woodstock, that, at its conclusion, they agreed never to give an interview or to speak of it again. That family pact remained true until 2008 when, as a widow, Clara Joyner finally consented to break her silence. Through her daughter, Ronnie, I caught up with Clara at her home in a northern suburb of Tampa, Florida. After showing off the new Mini-Cooper parked in her garage, she invited Ronnie and me into the living room of her impeccably clean yet New England furnished, southern ranch style home. Seemingly out of place down south, but not surprising, were the many Shaker and Adirondack style furnishings accompanying the family photos on the walls. Ronnie started by explaining to her mom that I was not there to challenge her beliefs or to judge her or her late husband. I shared with her the history and chronology of the Woodstock Program Project and it's intended significance. Slowly, over the course of the hour long discussion, Clara began to open up and let go of the long held family secrets. I chose my questions carefully. It didn't take long to realize just how culturally fearful the Joyners must have been when their quiet little world became the center of the universe for one very extended weekend. I let her page through the Program document in hopes that, in time, she would consent to adding her own signature. But it was clear from the onset that Clara's perspective on the event was light years away from mine. She remembered vividly how days before the concert officially started, hundreds of long-haired and dirty young people "invaded" the town and "cleaned us out of everything." She recounted how her husband Richard, who was already suffering from a weakened heart, was easily overwhelmed by the volume and cultural degradation of the clientel. When, on the Wednesday before the event, the Hells Angels showed up and threatened to burn down the building if the Joyners didn't co-operate with them, "Richard almost had another heart attack," Clara recalled. "Thank God we had another home, on Duggan Rd, about a mile south of the store. Every afternoon for the rest of the weekend, we would send our daughter home on foot, with a plain paper bag full of cash and receipts. If the bikers returned, they weren't getting the loot." As Clara spoke, I tried to put myself in her shoes during that historic week. As the owner of THE store of convenience to what everyone knew was going to be a monumental event, what would I do to prepare for the onslaught? There was more to this story than I realized and it would come to light in a most innocent manner toward the end of the interview when Clara told me that Richard was so unnerved by the whole experience that he and a group of other local merchants and farmers broke the code of brotherhood that had endured forever by blacklisting and ostracizing the Jewish farmer who, as they saw it, was personally responsible for the whole mess, Max Yasgur. That's right, Woodstock had accomplished the heretofore unthinkable; in only days, it had exposed the anti-Semitic underpinnings of a small rural and culturally diverse New York town and ended the farmers' code of mutual respect and cooperation. From that day until Max's passing, only a few years later, on February 9th, 1973, he was on his own. If he got his tractor stuck in the field during planting season, none of the area farmers, whom he had relied on before Woodstock, were there to pull him out. If Max needed assistance with milking or haying; sorry, you made your bed Mr. Yasgur! Clara seemed to profess her and Richard's actions without cognition or remorse and although the Joyners sold the store the following year, the seeds of a fractured and exposed community had been spread and would germinate for years to come. Max and Miriam's beautiful diary farm of rolling hills and spring- fed lakes would soon come face to face with its destiny.

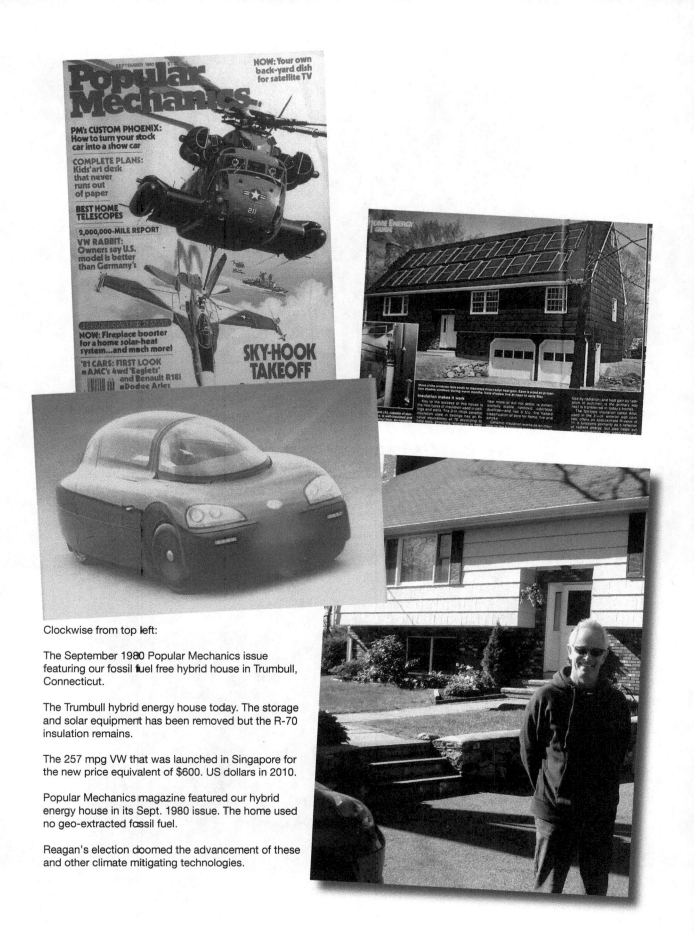

Clockwise from top left:

The September 1980 Popular Mechanics issue featuring our fossil fuel free hybrid house in Trumbull, Connecticut.

The Trumbull hybrid energy house today. The storage and solar equipment has been removed but the R-70 insulation remains.

The 257 mpg VW that was launched in Singapore for the new price equivalent of $600. US dollars in 2010.

Popular Mechanics magazine featured our hybrid energy house in its Sept. 1980 issue. The home used no geo-extracted fossil fuel.

Reagan's election doomed the advancement of these and other climate mitigating technologies.

Above, Early 1960's aerial photo of the Joyner's store with Esso gasoline sign.

Below, a 1920's oil painting of the Bethel General Store and Post Office by local artist Helen Lemon, given to the Joyner family by the store's previous owners.

Courtesy of Ronnie Joyner Hackett.

chapter ten
ARM UP WITH LOVE
AND COME FROM THE SHADOWS
–JOAN BAEZ

How many of you remember "Bloody Sunday"? If you grew up in the 60's you probably associate it with March 7th, 1965 when Alabama State and local police attacked a group of peaceful black local citizens who were protesting the coldblooded murder, a month earlier, of Jimmy Lee Jackson, a 26 year old church deacon, by James Fowler, an Alabama State Policeman. Jimmie Lee had tried unsuccessfully for four years to register to vote in his home town of Marion when he, his mother and his octogenarian grandmother were chased down by Alabama police and beaten to near death. As Jackson tried to protect his family, he was shot to death at point blank range kicking off the Selma Civil Rights marches one month later.

On Sunday, March 7th, six hundred marchers gathered on the Edmund Pettus Bridge in Selma, Alabama to demand justice for Jackson's murder and, inspired by Dr. Martin Luther King, seek a peaceful presence for civil liberty. Once again, Alabama authorities unleashed an unprovoked beating of a peaceful gathering that became known in American history as "Bloody Sunday." Justice for the Civil Rights Movement would be advanced only when the Federal Government stepped in on March 16th 1965 with 2,000 Army troops and 1,800 National Guard to guarantee that the protestors would achieve their goal of marching to Montgomery without harm.

How protracted is the advance of progress in America? James Fowler was not charged for his crime until May 10th, 2007. Forty-five years after killing an unarmed Jimmie Lee Jackson in cold blood, Fowler pleaded guilty to manslaughter on November 15th, 2010 and received a sentence of 6 months in prison. Nearly half a century after pulling the trigger, justice was still not served in the good old land of the free.

But wait. Did you know that there is another infamous "Bloody Sunday" civil rights massacre that took place during the Vietnam War era? It happened on Sunday January 30th, 1970. The facts about the Bogside Massacre are atrocious: 14 unarmed civil rights protesters shot and killed, by police. Two citizens run over by police vehicles, all victims unarmed. So why don't you know about this "Bloody Sunday"? Well, for one thing, it took place in Derry, Northern Ireland. But more importantly, it is no longer controversial because, unlike America's methodology, the British government has completed an extensive reinvestigation of the event and has made amends with all parties involved. Believe it.

Two days after Ireland's "Bloody Sunday," the Westminster Parliament convened a Tribunal of discovery. Within four years, the victims were found innocent of accusations that they had possessed explosives or firearms whilst being shot and by 1998 the Primer Minister of Britain, David Cameron, apologized to the British people at a meeting of The House of Commons, for the conduct of the British government on Bloody Sunday. When was the last time that the American government apologized for anything?

To be certain that justice was served, an additional seven year long "Saville Inquiry" interviewed more than 900 witnesses at a cost of 195 million pounds, making it the largest investigation in British legal history. The final report of the Saville was published on June 15, 2010 and concluded that "The firing by soldiers of 1PARA on Bloody Sunday caused the deaths of 13 people and injured a similar number, none of whom were posing a threat of causing death or serious injury." Saville further stated that British Paratroopers "Lost control," fatally shooting fleeing civilians and then concocting lies in an attempt to hide their acts.

On February 14th, 2013 the British government announced a settlement of 50,000 pounds sterling for each family seeking injury from the wrongful handling of Bloody Sunday.

"Where justice is denied, where poverty is enforced, where ignorance prevails, and where any one class is made to feel that society is an organized conspiracy to oppress, rob and degrade them, neither persons nor property will be safe."

Frederick Douglass

"Happiness is not a reward; it is a consequence. Suffering is not a punishment, it is a result."

Robert Greene Ingersoll

"The aim of art is to represent not the outward appearance of things, but their inward significance."

Aristotle

Courtesy of Miami University archives.

Police photo of Miami University student and ROTC protestor Myra Aronson (#13). On September 11, 2001 she was on board American Airlines Flight #11 that struck the World Trade Tower in New York City.

chapter eleven
FOUR DEAD IN OHIO – MAY 4TH, 1970

Having been tear gassed and having come so close to being murdered by my own government's militia during the anti-Vietnam War protests on Miami's campus, I remain deeply disturbed that, more than 40 years later, the families of the innocent victims and the American public alike have still been deprived of an un-censored and full scale investigation of the facts surrounding the Kent State Massacre of May 4th, 1970. How could 19 armed soldiers murder 4 unarmed students and wound many more at our sister college and walk away scott free? More importantly, how could the millions of patriotic and peace- loving citizens of our country ever find closure and forgiveness without an honest attempt at reconciliation and justice? Those of you for whom the details of the Kent State, May 4, 1970 Massacre have faded from or were not part of your personal memory, I submit the following recount from LiberationNews.Org.

The Ohio National Guard opened fire on a group of unarmed Kent State students, killing four and injuring nine. While the right-wing media tries to distort the truth of what took place on May 4, 1970, the true nature of the events reflects the significance of the anti-war movement during the Vietnam era.

Leading up to May 4,1970, the war had grown so unpopular

that even the right-wing imperialist Richard Nixon was forced to pledge an end to the Vietnam War if elected president. Congress had also created the draft lottery, which purported to end racial and class bias behind the draft. Further, soon after coming into office Nixon announced the withdrawal of 150,000 troops from Vietnam. This led some in establishment circles to hope that the anti-war movement would now wind down, along with the war.

All this changed on April 30, 1970, when President Nixon announced the invasion of Cambodia. This escalation rapidly reignited anti-war sentiment across the country. Shortly after the president's announcement, 200 State Department workers resigned, strikes spread across 60 campuses, and demonstrators stopped traffic in downtown Cincinnati.

On May 1, 1970, Students for a Democratic Society called for an anti-war demonstration in the middle of downtown Kent, Ohio, which would be followed by a massive rally on May 4.

The May 1 demonstration grew in size and militancy. On May 2, the local ROTC building was torched. The then-mayor of Kent, Leroy Satrom, contacted then-Governor James A. Rhodes in a panic. Gov. Rhodes ordered the National Guard to Kent and imposed martial law on the city.

The mayor, as well as the governor, used the media to attack protesters and sow division between the working-class residents of Kent and the students. The governor is quoted as saying, "They're worse than the brown shirts [Nazis] and the communist element and also the night riders [Ku Klux Klan] and the vigilantes."

While the media described the Kent State students as unruly, out of control and violent, violence did not begin until the National Guard arrived. The National Guard, along with help from the Kent Police Department, not only arrested hundreds of students within two days, but also beat and even bayoneted numerous citizens of the town.

The governor, the mayor and the dean of the university told the students that they must cancel the anti-war rally on May 4. They even forged fake flyers of the rally's cancellation in order to dissuade students from attending. Nevertheless, hundreds of students gathered in opposition to the invasion of Cambodia and the harsh treatment they had received at the hands of the authorities.

On May 4, the National Guard fired on unarmed student protesters.

The media immediately tried to spin the events that took place that day at Kent State. They portrayed the scenario as a standoff between the students and the National Guard. Video and photographs revealed what actually happened.

The National Guard killed two students, Sandra Scheuer and William Knox Schroeder, who were not even part of the demonstration. The nearest shooting victim, Joseph Lewis Jr., was about 60 feet away from the National Guard. The students posed no threat to the National Guard.

The Kent State shootings caused further unrest. Thirty-five college presidents called for withdrawal, while students at over 350 campuses launched strikes. Eventually, roughly 500 campuses closed down for some period of time, 50 for the remainder of the semester. In 16 states, the National Guard was mobilized to "keep order" on campuses.

Ten days after Kent State, Mississippi State troopers fired 300 bullets into a dormitory at historically black Jackson State University killing two, which sparked demonstrations on 50 campuses.

To this day, no member of the National Guard has ever been punished for the Kent State shootings. We deplore this lack of legal action, and further salute the students at Kent State who stood against the brutal imperialist war in Southeast Asia. The example of Kent State can show us that today, when the president claims to be winding down one war while escalating another, the role of the anti-war movement is as important as ever.

So, while the UK government apologized and brought reconciliation to British citizens for Bloody Sunday and the American government has done the same for the injustices it perpetrated on the black and civil rights protesters in Alabama and Mississippi on that Bloody Sunday, the brave anti-war students of America whose efforts ended one of the dark and treasonous moments in American presidential military history got snubbed, misrepresented and shut out of a judicial system meant to discover the truth and bring closure to those wronged on Kent States May 4th, "Bloody Monday." Only now, on March 15, 2013 as I am writing this, has it been officially reported by the BBC that, with the final release of the Lyndon Johnson White House tapes, Richard Nixon only created the illusion that he wanted to end the Vietnam War to win the election, while he was secretly sending messages to Hanoi to walk away from the Paris Peace talks. Tricky Dick promised them a better deal when he won the election. Twenty two thousand more American soldiers died as a direct result of Nixon's treasonous charade. That was the better deal that we protesters and other true American heroes fought so hard to prevent. Millions of patriots, young and old, put their lives on the line to end the massacre, culminating in Nixon's resignation and yet, not one bridge or highway is named for their effort and sacrifice. Please log on to your favorite social network and make your voice heard.

Top: Kent State students standing or walking in this parking lot were gunned down by National Guardsmen located on the distant ridge beyond the trees .

Left: The Guardsmen's view, taking aim at innocent students, many greater than 100 yards away.

Bottom: Lighted piers surrounding sight of the fallen student victim who was closest to National Guard.

237

The Kent State Museum features the Original Woodstock poster in its main lobby.

chapter twelve
E=MC²

According to Einstein's Special Theory of Relativity, time diverges universally away from each of us at a speed of 186,000 miles per second, give or take. E=MC2 simply means, energy = mass x the velocity of light (time) squared. That energy coalesces with all other energy in a kind of inter-galactic dance to which we each contribute. It's a beautiful thing to be part of, but it also means that you cannot go back and re-live the past; contrary to Hollywood fantasy. The Woodstock Program Project has never been about missing or re-living Woodstock. That moment and its energy are now part of the dance. In truth, it's really about continuing to dance each and every day. I intend to keep chasing Woodstock until its 50th Anniversary; that would be August 2019. At that time, it is my hope that The Program and its provenance be returned to the spot of its journey's beginning and put on display so that each and every one of you can see it as a symbol of the love and peace that our nation finds so difficult to embrace. Mr. Gerry, it's time for you to relinquish your personal financial interest in Bethel Woods, and give the Garden back to All the People in the form of a National Historical Park that would be the site of America's first true monument to and for Peace. We sure could use your help re-naming all the Sullivan County roads and bridges that were impacted by Woodstock's traffic after people, artists, songs, groups, symbols and ethos etc., each sign pointing the way. A significant contribution toward the erection of the Monument itself wouldn't hurt. What do you say Mr. Gerry? Are you in?

Recently, Linda and I have found ourselves quoting lines from the classic movie "Pretty Woman" with our friend Andy. It has become our "bible" for almost every situation in life and seems to offer an enlightened answer. "Everyone has a dream! What's your dream?" Here's mine. You know the scene where Edward Lewis (Richard Gere) asks everyone to leave the boardroom so that he can speak privately and honestly with Mr. Morris (Ralph Bellamy) the man who's ship building business he had intended to acquire, then dismantle? Remember what Mr. Morris says to Edward after Mr. Lewis informs him that he wishes to help him grow his business rather than take it over and break it up? Morris looks at Edward with renewed affection and says, " I don't know how to say this without sounding condescending, but I'm proud of you." This is the pivotal moment in the movie when the confluence of two opposing philosophies find common humanistic objective. In my version, I get to pat Alan Gerry on the back and utter the same line.

I'll see you all at America's first true monument to peace and music, "The Woodstock National Historical Peace Park and Monument" in Bethel, New York on the weekend of August 16, 17 & 18, 2019 for the dedication. It's time to create a place where future generations of children and adults can go to learn the lessons of basic and shared human values.

Bring your camping gear, food to share and a change of clothes.
It could get muddy.

the end

Woodstock's legendary mud at the 25th anniversary celebration.

THE AFFIRMATIONS OF HUMANISM

by Paul Kurtz.

We are committed to the application of reason and science to the understanding of the universe and to the solving of human problems.

We deplore efforts to denigrate human intelligence, to seek to explain the world in supernatural terms and to look outside nature for salvation.

We believe in an open and pluralistic society and that democracy is the best guarantee of protecting human rights from authoritarian elites and repressive majorities.

We are committed to the principle of the separation of church and state.

We cultivate the arts of negotiation and compromise as a means of resolving differences and achieving mutual understanding.

We are concerned with securing justice and fairness in society and with eliminating discrimination and intolerance.

We believe in the common moral decencies: altruism, integrity, honesty, truthfulness and responsibility. Humanist ethics is amenable to critical, rational guidance. There are normative standards that we discover together. Moral principles are tested by their consequences.

We attempt to transcend divisive parochial loyalties based on race, religion, gender, nationality, creed, class, sexual orientation or ethnicity and strive to work together for the common good of humanity.

We affirm humanism as a realistic alternative to theologies of despair and ideologies of violence and as a source of rich personal significance and genuine satisfaction in the service of others.

We believe in optimism rather than pessimism, hope rather than despair, learning in the place of dogma, truth instead of ignorance, joy rather than guilt or sin, tolerance in the place of fear, LOVE instead of hatred, compassion over selfishness, beauty instead of ugliness and reason rather than blind faith and irrationality.

We believe in the fullest realization of the best and noblest that we are capable of as human beings.*

©The Council for Secular Humanism, used by permission.

Non-theists are the fastest growing segment of the American population today. To read more, go to SecularHumanism.org.

THREE STEPS TO FREEDOM IN AMERICA

1.   Take an honest and critical look at the legacy of organized religion, especially your own, if you are a follower. Talk to family and friends about your concerns. We must begin an open dialogue if we are to advance as a people, beyond first century ideology.

2.   Vote for representatives who commit themselves to the principle of governance of the people, by the people and for the people. Candidates who represent the needs of special interests and the privileged 2%, including monopolistic mega corporations (which, contrary to the Supreme Court of our land, are not people), must be replaced by those willing to fight for the social and moral values that are beneficial to ALL. The last time there was this much of an imbalance in the distribution of money and power in America, F.D.R. introduced The New Deal. It was a resounding success.

   Our 21st Century New Deal is simple. Bust ALL corporations deemed too big to fail or having more than 100,000 employees, for example, then require all businesses with more than 100 employees to become employee owned and operated. Employees do not make decisions that will hurt them personally.

3. Demand that your elected representatives convert our military aggression worldwide into diplomacy worldwide, while maintaining our defensive technological vigilance and superiority. We have no more right to invade other countries than they have to invade ours. And having a two party political system does not mandate that one of those parties has to be philosophically Regressive. America's future lies with a strong Democratic and a stronger Progressive ideology. Vote for America's future. Vote for your future. Vote for your family's future. Join me and vote America back from the plutocratic Stratocracy it has become, to the Nomocracy it was always intended to be…a concept worth chasing.

This is how simple it is to return America to a democracy of, by and for the people, but we must have the will to advance ourselves as a nation, ONE PROGRESSIVE NATION, period.

HOW TO BUILD COMMUNITY

Turn off your TV. Leave your house. Know your neighbors. Greet people. Look up when you're walking. Sit on the stoop. Plant flowers. Use your library. Play together. Buy from local merchants. Share what you have. Help a lost dog. Take children to the park. Honor elders. Support neighborhood schools. Fix it even if you didn't break it. Have pot lucks. Garden together. Pick up litter. Read stories aloud. Dance in the streets. Talk to the mail carrier. Listen to the birds. Put up a swing. Help carry something heavy. Barter for your goods. Start a tradition. Ask a question. Hire young people for odd jobs. Organize a block party. Bake extra and share. Ask for help when you need it. Open your shades. Sing together. Share your skills. Take back the night. Turn up the music. Turn down the music. Listen before you react to anger. Mediate a conflict. Seek to understand. Learn from new and uncomfortable angles. Know that no one is silent though many are not heard. Work to change this.

Used by permission – Syracuse Cultural Workers, Publisher of Peace and Justice since 1982

ACKNOWLEDGMENTS

The author insists on thanking the following friends and fellow Homo sapiens for their creative contributions...

Alan & Iris Evans

Ken and Maggie Evans

Catherine Evans Hourigan

Patricia Kiracofe

Professor emeritus, Author and uncle Milton White

Kevin, "The Mayor of Woodstock" Bowman

Andrew Singer, Friend and fellow audiophile

Yvonne Daley, Author and director of Vermont

Writers Conference

Dell Aitchison second proofing

Valerie Elliott, Head of Smith Library of Regional History, Oxford, Ohio 45056

Jim & Jackie Shulman, Professional advisers

Betty Moffett, Inspirational friend and author

Sheridan Elementary School, Class of 1962, Bridgeport, Connecticut

Dave Morello, Tech master extraordinaire

Emmilee Smith - Cover Swirl

Austin Farrell, InDesign creative formatting.

Nic Gillam, InDesign creative formatting.

Linda Kiracofe Evans for virtually everything else.

Scooby & The Father for making 50 Peet Street a grrreat place to grow up!

CPSIA information can be obtained
at www.ICGtesting.com
Printed in the USA
JSHW040332170222
22949JS00003B/34